THE TIGER TANK

ROGER FORD

THE TIGER TANK

ROGER FORD

SPELLMOUNT
Staplehurst

British Library Cataloguing in Publication Data:
A catalogue record for this book is available
from the British Library

ISBN 1-86227-030-9

First published in the UK in 1998 by
Spellmount Limited
The Old Rectory
Staplehurst
Kent TN12 0AZ

1 3 5 7 9 8 6 4 2

Editorial and design: Brown Packaging Books Ltd
Bradley's Close, 74-77 White Lion Street,
London N1 9PF

Editor: Anne Cree
Design: Jane Felstead

Printed and bound in the Czech Republic

Picture credits
Christopher Ailsby Historical Archives: 82-83
IWM: 12, 22, 23, 26, 29, 33, 38, 39, 53, 66, 72 (b), 88, 89, 90 (both)
MARS: 14-15
John Norris: 25, 32
Tank Museum Collection, Bovington: 13, 27, 31, 34-35, 46, 51, 52, 57, 60, 67
(both), 71 (both), 73 (b), 80, 84-85
TRH Pictures: 8 (both), 44-45, 47, 50 (t), 56, 58, 59, 62-63, 68, 69, 70, 73 (t),
77, 81 (both)
TRH Pictures via Espadon: 20, 21, 61, 72 (t), 78
Martin Windrow: 6-7, 10-11, 17, 24, 28, 30, 32, 40, 41, 42, 48 (both), 50 (b),
64-65, 65, 76

Artwork credits
John Batchelor: 54-55, 74 (both), 86
Bob Garwood: 75 (both)
Ray Hutchins: 18-19, 36-37
Salamander Picture Library: 87

Pages 2-3: Tigers of *schwere SS-Panzer Abteilung* 101, *Leibstandarte*
Division, on their way to the front in Normandy in June 1944.

CONTENTS

CHAPTER 1

Genesis of the Tiger

Germany was late in developing armoured fighting vehicles, but wasted no time in catching, and then surpassing, her rivals. After several false starts, the design for the Tiger – the heavy tank which Hitler insisted was the only sure battle-winner – was finalised in early 1941, and the tank went to war less than six months later.

During World War I, the German High Command paid only scant and belated attention to the development of armoured fighting vehicles. Cumbersome A7V *Sturmpanzerwagen* 'tanks' (as the British had called their first such experiments, in an attempt to hide their real purpose) were produced in very small numbers. Out of a total of 20, only 15 saw action – and were never effective. In the first ever tank-v-tank battle, near Villers-Bretonneux on 24 April 1918, two were destroyed and a third overturned in its haste to escape – though to be fair, 'haste' is a relative term: the vehicle's top speed, even under ideal conditions, was just 9kmph (5.6mph). This happened after the tanks had engaged two machine-gun-armed Female Mark IVs and were surprised by the appearance of a Male Mark IV, with its more potent twin six-pounder guns.

By that time, however – and despite initial setbacks – the real tactical value of the new weapon had been established well enough, during the British attack on Cambrai in November 1917. Ultimately, the 474 Mark IV tanks committed there were driven back, but not before they had proved that they could break the deadlock imposed by the combination of barbed wire and machine guns which had ruled the battlefield for three long, bloody years.

In 1918, German engineers started work on new tanks – the giant, 150-tonne (147-ton) K-wagen (*Grosskampfwagen*), with a crew of no less than 22 men, armed with four 7.7cm guns and seven 7.92mm machine guns, and powered by two 650hp aero engines, two prototypes of which were partially completed. Work had also begun on the diminutive LK (*Leichter Kampfwagen*) series, based on the chassis of a Daimler touring car. The light tank programme culminated in the LK II, a nine-tonne (9.14-ton), three-man tank, armed with a 5.7cm

Left: A pristine Tiger rolls out of the Kassel factory, February 1942, minus its outer roadwheels and on narrow tracks, ready for loading aboard a train. The mudguards have yet to be fitted, as does the hull machine gun.

Above: Tiger tanks taking part in an exercise in Germany. The heavy duty torsion bar suspension of the Tiger ensured a smooth ride, even at speed over rough country – and despite the tank's weight. Note the difference in deflection between the running gear of the two vehicles.

Below: The PzKpfw V Panther (such as this *Ausführung* D, pictured at the Henschel proving grounds in mid-1943) and the PzKpfw VI Tiger had much in common but were essentially different in character, although the Panther was much more cost-effective (and not much less battleworthy) than the Tiger.

cannon in a fixed barbette and a single 7.92mm machine gun. It was a response to the introduction by the British of the generally similar – though heavier and, hence, less manoeuvrable – Medium Tank Mark A, known as the Whippet.

The LK II showed some promise, and its two prototypes performed well enough for 580 of them to be ordered, but they arrived too late to see action. The design was later sold to Sweden, where it was modified by the addition of a rotating turret, now with a 37mm gun, and put into production in 1924–25 as the *Stridsvagn* Strv. m/21. It was in one of these Swedish tanks that Heinz Guderian got his first hands-on experience of the weapon he was to wield so effectively, when he was allowed to drive one during an official visit to Sweden in the spring of 1929. Guderian was eventually to become one of the most effective armoured force commanders of all time.

CIRCUMVENTING THE VERSAILLES TREATY

Sweden was a good friend of Germany in those days. The Versailles Treaty of 1919, which formally ended World War I, forbade Germany from possessing, developing or manufacturing weapons of many types, including, not too surprisingly, armoured fighting vehicles. (It also forbade many more mundane weapons: pistols with barrels longer than 100mm [4in], for example.) Hitler unilaterally revoked the treaty when the Nazis came to power in 1933, but until that time Germany relied on clandestine help from foreign countries in its attempt to rebuild the armaments industry which the Allies had dismantled in 1919.

Sweden was one of the countries that gave help, though on a much smaller scale than Denmark, Holland and Switzerland. But by far the most important was the Soviet Union, where Germany had access to the tank-proving ground at Kazan, east of the Ural Mountains and virtually hidden from prying Western eyes. It was here that a new generation of German tanks was tested, and where German engineering know-how was applied to good effect in the parallel development of a new armoured force for the Soviets. It is one of the ironies of history that less than two decades later those two countries were to fight the biggest tank battle ever.

The first German tanks tested under this arrangement were the *Leichter Traktor* from Krupp and Rheinmetall (the companies built three prototypes each, to an identical overall specification), each of which weighed in at 10 tonnes (9.84 tons) and resembled a British Medium Mark II, with its 3.7cm gun in a revolving turret, and the *Grosstraktor*, this time in three versions, from Daimler-Benz, Krupp, and Rheinmetall, which was 7.2 tonnes (seven tons) heavier and armed with either a 7.5cm gun or a 10.5cm howitzer. In 1933, these two tanks were followed by the *Neubaufahrzeug* (new construction vehicle) generally referred to in print by its acronym: PzKw NbFz.

Krupp, MAN (Maschinenfabrik Augsburg-Nürnberg) and Rheinmetall all bid for the contract to design the hull of the NbFz, which finally went to Rheinmetall, while Krupp and Rheinmetall both submitted designs for turrets. Rheinmetall designed a turret with superimposed coaxially mounted 10.5cm and 3.7cm weapons, which was to be realised as the NbFz B, and Krupp designed a turret with side-by-side coaxial 7.5cm and 3.7cm guns, as the NbFz A. Both versions mounted two additional smaller turrets, identical to those fitted to the PzKpfw (*Panzerkampfwagen*) (K) I light tank (see below), one forward and the other aft of the main turret and offset to right and left respectively, and both armed with paired 7.92mm machine guns.

THE EARLY PANZERS

Neither version was either practical or popular; indeed, the multiple-turret concept, which requires both additional crewmen and inevitably introduces shot-traps, had actually been discredited by the time they came into service. Few were produced, and they were only ever used in the training role, though some turned up during the invasion of Norway in the spring of 1940, and caused some confusion in Allied intelligence-gathering circles. They were originally given the designations PzKpfw V and PzKpfw VI (see box on this page on how to decode the sometimes rather complex system the German Army used to denominate its vehicles), which led to some later confusion, since those two designations were also given to the tanks we know best as the Panther and the Tiger.

These tanks were obsolescent, a throwback to an earlier age, and, even while they were going into production, the German High Command was formulating an overall tactical plan which simply ignored them. This plan called for light and medium tanks to be formed into armoured divisions and employed together according to a rigid set of rules. The first new vehicle to be developed under this plan – in 1934 – was the Krupp-designed LaS A or PzKw IA, later known as the PzKpfw IA (SdKfz 101). At this time, German tanks were thinly disguised by being referred to as LaS – *landwirtschaftliche Schlepper* – agricultural tractors. This was a five-tonne (4.92-ton), two-man tank with a maximum of 13mm (fractionally over 0.5in) of armour, powered by a four-cylinder, air-cooled 60hp Krupp M105 petrol engine, which gave it a top speed on the road of 40kmph (25mph) and a range of 150km (90 miles). It was armed with two 7.92mm machine guns, which meant it was effective only against unprotected infantry and soft-skinned vehicles.

The PzKpfw IA had suspension which was barely adequate, even for the tank's low all-up weight. This was the first thing to be modified in the light of operational experience,

ARMOURED VEHICLE NOMENCLATURE

The second-generation tanks (*Panzerkampfwagen*) with which Germany fought World War II were initially abbreviated as 'PzKw', but this caused confusion, since personnel carriers were known by the abbreviation 'PKw'. Armoured fighting vehicles thus came to be designated 'PzKpfw' or 'Pz.Kpfw', though not until halfway through the war. A Roman numeral was used to distinguish one vehicle type from another – PzKpfw IV, for example – and models or versions were distinguished by a capital-letter alphabetic *Ausführung* number, usually abbreviated to Ausf.

In addition, all vehicles of the German armed services received a unique SdKfz (*Sonderkraftfahrzeug* – special purpose vehicle) number, which did not change from one version to the next. Thus, all 12 versions of the PzKpfw III were known as SdKfz 141. The number only changed if a major variant was produced.

The last three German tanks of World War II also received names – Tiger, Panther and Tiger II, the latter also widely known as the King Tiger (*Königstiger*). Thus they became, for example, PzKpfw V Panther Ausf G. Some tanks' designations were changed retroactively – the PzKpfw VI Tiger Ausf H (SdKfz 181) was later redesignated as the PzKpfw VI Tiger I Ausf E, for example. The Tiger II eventually lost its Roman-numeral type designator, becoming the PzKpfw Tiger II Ausf B (SdKfz 182). The Ausf. designators were not always allocated in alphabetical order, nor did they use all the letters of the alphabet. In the case of the Tiger, the original Ausf suffixes (H and P) actually refer to the designers, Henschel and Porsche. Subvariants sometimes received an Arabic numeral after the alphabetic designator: PzKpfw IV Ausf F2, for example.

Tanks of the same type but with different guns were differentiated by a reference to the main weapon, either its nominal calibre, its own type designator or even by the length of its barrel. Thus, a PzKpfw III with the short-barrelled 7.5cm gun might be referred to as a PzKpfw III (75). Tigers were often differentiated from King Tigers by reference to their main guns. The Tiger became PzKpfw VI (8.8cm KwK 36 L/56) and the King Tiger, PzKpfw VI (8.8cm KwK 43 L/71). Any unique sub-designator was used, so long as it assisted vehicle identification.

From 1938, prototype and experimental tanks first received a 'VK' (*Vollkettenkraftfahrzeug* – full-tracked motor vehicle) designator, followed by a four-digit number, the first pair of which described its weight in tonnes, while the second pair differentiated one prototype from another. When an identical specification was given to two or more manufacturers, a simple abbreviation of their name was appended, in brackets: VK 3001 (H), for example, for a tank developed by Henschel.

From 1943 onwards, experimental tanks and those under development got a simpler 'E' (for *Entwicklungstyp* – development type) designation, followed by an approximate weight-class.

Author's note: To aid clarity, I use the name 'Tiger' to mean the PzKpfw VI Tiger I Ausf. H/E, (SdKfz 181) with the L/56 KwK 36 gun, and the name King Tiger to mean the PzKpfw Tiger II Ausf B Königstiger, (SdKfz 182) with the L/71 KwK 43 gun.

and the PzKpfw IB, which followed at the end of 1934, also gained a six-cylinder 100hp Maybach NL38TR petrol engine, but otherwise its operating characteristics were little changed. These tanks saw active service during the Spanish Civil War and later during the invasions of Poland, the Low Countries and France, by which time they were obsolete and were withdrawn into support roles.

The development of the medium tank planned to operate alongside the Panzer Mark I was delayed, and it was joined instead by an interim design, the LaS 100 PzKpfw II, with

That was just as well, for it was 1937 before the medium tanks started to roll off the production lines. These were the excellent 21-tonne (20.6-ton) PzKpfw III, designed by Daimler-Benz and modified by Krupp, and the 23-tonne (22.63-ton) PzKpfw IV, designed by Krupp and modified by Rheinmetall. They were known initially as the *Zugführerswagen* (troop commander's vehicle) and *Bataillonführerswagen* (battalion commander's vehicle) – like 'LaS', the designations were meant to confuse.

These tanks, and particularly the latter, with its larger turret ring, also proved capable of considerable improvement in terms of both their offensive equipment and their defensive capabilities: the amount of armour they could carry without becoming dangerously overweight. But even in the year of their launch there was a growing conviction that they would eventually prove inadequate in a war which was already seen as inevitable.

PROTOTYPE HEAVY TANKS

This quite justified fear led to a further design study, for a 30-tonne- (29.52-ton-) plus vehicle. In 1937 the contract to build a prototype was awarded to Henschel u. Söhne, which, up until that time, had been conspicuously absent from the field. No sooner had testing of the hull/chassis of the first Henschel DW 1 (for *Durchbruchswagen* – breakthrough vehicle) begun the following year, than the work was halted. Henschel was now instructed to start work on a much bigger vehicle instead: the 65-tonne (64-ton) VK 6501, which was in many respects an evolution of the NbFz, complete with its discredited auxiliary machine-gun turrets. Henschel completed two prototypes before the VK 6501 was cancelled in its turn in 1940, and the company was told to start work again on a tank in the 30-tonne (29.5-ton) class, to be known now as the DW 2.

This programme too was halted, in 1941, in favour of a new design in the same general class. Proposals were submitted by Daimler-Benz, MAN and Porsche, as well as by Henschel, and the two latter companies were instructed to produce four prototypes each, which were to be known as the VK 3001 (P) and the VK 3001 (H) respectively. Meanwhile work on a 36-tonne (35.5-ton) tank (VK 3601), to be armed with an innovative squeeze-bore 7.5cm gun also began. That gun – which would have had the same destructive power as the 8.8cm gun described below, while allowing a much greater quantity of ammunition to be stored in the same space – was eventually abandoned because its projectile was formed from tungsten, which was in increasingly short supply by that time. However, the project continued with a conventional long-barrelled KwK (*Kampfwagenkanone*) 42 7.5cm gun in its place.

The VK 3001 (H) was orthodox in every way; it was similar in appearance to the PzKpfw IV, but had the seven medium-diameter roadwheel layout conceived for the VK 6501. Dr Ferdinand Porsche's submission, which he called the Leopard, was outwardly similar but less conventional, having longitudinal torsion bars and petrol-electric drive, whereby the main engine drove a generator, which in turn provided power to electric motors to drive each track. The idea was not novel by any

heavier armour, a more powerful Maybach engine, and a 2cm cannon in place of one of its machine guns. The Mark II proved to be a rugged vehicle, capable of considerable further development – a factor which Britain and France, in particular, failed to take into account in their own tank programmes.

Above: This *Ausführung* E Tiger – captured intact by the British and later put on public display – shows a common field modification: the spare track links carried on the lower front plate, acting as (ineffective) extra armour.

means, and had the huge advantage of simplifying enormously the complex problem of steering the tank, but it did mean large power losses and had other, more far-reaching drawbacks.

Henschel's four prototype VK 3001s appeared in pairs, in March and October 1941. They were armed – as were all the German heavy-tank designs up to that point – with the KwK 43 L/43, a longer-barrelled version of the 7.5cm low-velocity gun fitted to the early versions of the PzKpfw IV. They proved to be competent designs in mechanical terms, but while the testing programme progressed through the spring and summer, doubts began to grow as reports started to filter back from the battlefields of the Soviet Union of the battle-fitness of those selfsame PzKpfw IVs.

With their frontal armour just 30mm (1.2in) thick, they were proving themselves extremely vulnerable to the Soviet tanks they were encountering as Operation 'Barbarossa' rolled eastwards. At the same time their 7.5cm L/24 guns, which fired a 6.75kg (15lb) APCBC (armour-piercing, capped, ballistic-capped) round at a muzzle velocity of 385m/sec (1265 ft/sec), could not penetrate the enemy tanks' 45mm- (1.8in-) thick sloping frontal armour at anything other than suicidally close range.

On 20 November 1941, any residual optimism that might have remained was dashed when a German engineering investigation team was able to examine one of the new Soviet T-34s, which had been captured more or less intact. Within days the VK 3001/VK 3601 programme was scrapped, and all available resources were directed instead towards developing a heavier tank, with very much better protection and a gun capable of penetrating 100mm (3.9in) of armour at a range of 1500m (1640yds), thus able to defeat the enemy at stand-off range outside the effective range of his armament.

With the benefit of hindsight, there must be some question as to the overall wisdom of that decision, for the 30-tonne (29.5-ton) tank programme was later revived, and a design proposed by MAN was eventually to become the PzKpfw V Panther (SdKfz 171), which many consider to have been the

best all-round German tank of World War II despite its disappointing beginnings. This raises a very interesting question: was the Tiger tank the right vehicle to put into production at that time, intended as it was to fight in Russia? Or was it chosen in deference to Hitler's personal bias towards weapons of pronounced size and weight?

THE FIRST TIGER

The decision to develop a tank in the 45-tonne (44.3-ton) class, rather than a much lighter vehicle, was influenced by the fact that a considerable amount of work on a heavier tank had already been completed, since prototypes of the VK 4501 had been ordered from both Henschel and Porsche the previous May. Essentially, these were uprated VK 3001s, incorporating the running gear – large interleaved roadwheels – developed for the DW 2, and 8.8cm KwK 36 L/56 guns, developed from the very successful 8.8cm FlaK (*Fliegerabwehrkanone* – anti-aircraft gun) 18. The KwK 36 cannon fired either a 10kg (22lb) Pzgr.39 (*Panzergranate*) APCBC projectile at a muzzle velocity of 773m/sec (2535ft/sec) or a lighter, 7kg (16lb) tungsten-cored Pzgr.40 round at 930m/sec (3050ft/sec). Either projectile was capable of penetrating a T-34's frontal armour at ranges in excess of 2000m (2190yds). In order to incorporate the desired level of protection, the prototypes exceeded their design weight, in the case of the Henschel variant by as much as 11 tonnes (10.8 tons), while neither had a more powerful engine than that originally specified.

The first examples were to be ready to be presented to the Führer on 20 April 1942 – his 53rd birthday. Both Henschel and Porsche met the schedule, and production orders were placed for both variants of what was to become known as the

Above: A tank from *3.Kompanie schwere Panzer-Abteilung 503* (its tactical number is obscured here) demonstrates its obstacle-crossing capabilities to officers of Germany's allies – the branches were picked up on the way, not applied as an attempt at camouflage!

PzKpfw VI Tiger – the first German tank to receive an official name. The order for the Porsche variant – for just 90 vehicles – was an insurance in case Henschel failed to deliver the preferred tank as planned. In the event, it soon became obvious that there were no production problems at the Henschel plant at Kassel, and the Porsche Tiger metamorphosed while still unfinished into the *Elefant Panzerjäger* (tank destroyer) with a fixed gun. We shall consider the *Elefant* further in Chapter Five.

In the spring of 1942, two prototypes as well as one production tank (three others followed at irregular intervals) were delivered to the German Army for trials. In mid-August 1942 the first four production PzKpfw IV Tiger Ausf H (SdKfz 181) heavy tanks, enough to equip just one platoon, were shipped to 1 Company/502nd Heavy Tank Battalion, and the unit – which also operated PzKpfw IIIs – was despatched from its depot at Fallingbostel by train. It arrived at the Eastern Front on 29 August to join Army Group North in the area south of Lake Ladoga, on the eastern side of Leningrad. There, during the first week of September 1942, a single Tiger, the other three being temporarily out of commission, made its operational debut on an uneventful security patrol.

Design and Layout of the Tiger Tank

The Tiger was the first German tank of World War II to have been designed with the benefit of real combat experience. Despite its size, accommodation was cramped, in both hull and turret, and access was difficult, but what it lacked in comfort it made up for in security and firepower, as its armour was the thickest, and its gun the most powerful, the world had ever seen.

Hitler's ultimate requirement for what was to become the PzKpfw VI Tiger (SdKfz 181) heavy tank was quite simple and straightforward: the vehicle to be developed was to dominate the battlefield, not just as it existed in late 1941, but for the foreseeable future. Of course, it was one thing for him to demand a tank capable of defeating all comers, and quite another actually to define, develop and realise such a vehicle, especially in the short time that the Führer's deadline allowed. In this, Germany was very fortunate in having one of the most talented engineers in the field – H.E. Kniepkamp – who had overall responsibility for the development of tracked vehicles. Kniepkamp had been in charge of Germany's armoured vehicle programme long before it became public knowledge, and by 1942, at the age of 47, he was at the peak of his considerable ability. Clearly, such a massive undertaking as the development of an all-new heavy tank has to be the work of many men, but equally clearly Kniepkamp's contribution stands out. It even extended into the design of the HL210/230 series engines and the innovative OLVAR semi-automatic transmission and its associated regenerative steering gear.

TO DEFEAT ALL-COMERS

Of course, Germany was not alone in having talented tank designers. The Soviet Union had its share, in particular, M.I. Koshkin, until his death in 1940, and A.A. Morozov, Koshkin's pupil and successor as Chief Designer at Tankograd, as the USSR's armoured-vehicle development establishment at Chelyabinsk became known. The T-34

Left: Hitler's Asian Axis allies showed some interest in acquiring Tigers, and in the autumn of 1943 a group of Japanese officers travelled to Germany to see the giant tank for themselves. One vehicle was actually earmarked for shipment to Tokyo that October, but was diverted to *s.SS-Pz.Abt. 101* instead.

GUN NOMENCLATURE

It was German practice during World War II to describe small arms – pistols, rifles and machine guns – by the calibre of their bore, expressed in millimetres, 9mm and 7.92mm, for example. Larger-calibre guns were denominated in centimetres, 7.5cm, for example, or 8.8cm, while the practice of other nations was to use millimetres, for example, the American 75mm M3. However, British tanks and anti-tank guns (as well as some artillery pieces) were distinguished by the weight of the projectile they fired, in pounds – the six-pounder and 17-pounder, for example – though some older types were known by the diameter of their bore in either inches or millimetres.

The term 'calibre' refers to the bore of the barrel, usually (but by no means exclusively) excluding the rifling. Thus, we refer to a 7.92mm-calibre MG34 medium machine gun, or a Browning GP35 pistol in 9mm Parabellum calibre. (Small arms ammunition is often known by its calibre and cartridge length together – 7.92mm x 57, for example, or by suffixing the calibre with a common name, such as Parabellum or ACP – as there are many variations in a single calibre.)

With small arms, the term calibre has no other meaning. Within artillery – including tanks and even naval guns – it is also used to describe the length of the bore of a gun's barrel. (The Americans measure this length from the rear of the chamber to the muzzle; the Germans, from the rear of the breech to the muzzle. Where a muzzle brake is fitted, it is not counted in either figure.) Thus, a gun of 56 calibres (often expressed as L/56), has a barrel 56 times as long as its nominal bore. In the KwK 36 8.8cm L/56 gun, this means a total barrel length (including breech) of 56 x 8.8cm, or 4.93m (16.2ft).

Rifle and machine-gun calibre ammunition comes in many forms, including incendiary and explosive types, though jacketed hard point (JHP), jacketed soft point (JSP), tracer and armour-piercing (AP) are the most common. Ammunition for anti-tank guns and armoured vehicles' own main armament is available in a wider range. For the Tiger, three types of 8.8cm ammunition were provided: armour-piercing, high explosive (HE) and high-explosive anti-tank (HEAT). The most common variety of AP was the Pzgr.39, a 10.2kg (22.44lb) armour-piercing capped, ballistic-capped round with an explosive filling which left the KwK36's muzzle at a velocity of 773m/sec (2535ft/sec).

AP rounds normally accounted for 50 per cent of a Tiger's ammunition load, the rest being taken up with Sprgr. HE rounds for use against soft-skinned vehicles and troop formations. The hollow-charge Gr.39HL round, which was less effective at short range, but retained penetrating power as it was not dependent on kinetic energy, was sometimes substituted for some of the HE load though it was much less accurate. The Pzgr.39 APCBC round was capable of penetrating 120mm (4.72in) of armour set at an angle of 30 degrees at a range of 1000m (1090yds), and 84mm (3.3in) of armour at 2000m (2180yds); the tungsten-cored Pzgr.40 round could penetrate 170mm (6.7in) of armour at short range and 110mm (4.3in) at 2000m (2180yds), while the Gr.39HL round could penetrate 90mm (3.5in) of armour up to a maximum of 2000m (2180yds).

which Koshkin began and Morozov brought to production was very obviously the outstanding armoured vehicle of the day, and, many would maintain, the best all-round tank of World War II, particularly in its later form, with the 85mm gun. The T-34 was the new German tank's chief adversary, and its defeat was its short-term objective. The operating capabilities and characteristics of the T-34 therefore clearly played a large part in defining and setting the minimum requirements of the new tank, but, equally clearly, the Tiger far exceeded them.

The new German tank – the first since World War I to be designed with the benefit of real combat experience, leaving aside the somewhat misleading lessons of the Spanish Civil War – was to come out at over twice the weight of the early T-34/76A, with armour over twice as thick. Its main gun, the 8.8cm L/56 KwK 36 could perforate (that is, pass entirely through) 138mm (5.5in) of homogeneous armour set at a 30-degree angle, at a distance of 1000m (1090yds). By contrast, the early T-34's 76.2mm L/30.5 M1938 L-11 could perforate 58mm (2.3in) of armour at a similar range and angle; the slightly superior L/41.5 M1940 F-34 gun, introduced in 1942, could perforate 67mm (2.65in).

THE TIGER'S ADVERSARIES

The Tiger was thus conceived not just to beat the T-34, but to go one clear step further, thanks to levels of protection and firepower that were markedly superior to anything ever seen before. In fact, the vehicle's sheer physical size, complexity and weight, and the amount it cost to manufacture as a result, ensured that it would never be more than an occasional player. (The nominal cost of a Tiger was 250,000 Reichsmarks, though that does not take account of such factors as the use of slave labour. In contrast, a PzKpfw III cost RM96,200, a PzKpfw IV RM103,500 and a Panther RM117,000; all these figures are exclusive of weapons and radios.) There were over 25 times as many T-34s manufactured as there were Tigers, and almost 35 times as many Shermans. Nevertheless, whenever the Tiger appeared it dominated the battlefield, right up to the last days of the war.

Of course, no sooner did the Tiger emerge than steps were taken to produce tanks able to stand up to it. The IS series from the Soviet Union relied on brute force, with heavy armour and a gun even more powerful than the KwK 36. This soon forced the Tiger onto the defensive – where, perversely, it was at its best anyway, being far too ponderous to fight a successful fire-and-movement battle. Meanwhile, the M26 Pershing from the USA and the British A34 Comet took a middle course, with less substantial armour and a somewhat inferior gun but with considerably better performance. These latter came too late to solve the Tiger problem in Western Europe, and the Allies had to rely on the rather risky tactic of massing Shermans and other less competitive vehicles, in the manner of dogs set upon a bull, and often at considerable cost in lives. The breakthrough came thanks to a vast superiority in numbers, not thanks to the superior qualities of US or British tanks.

Superior protection and devastating firepower, the two factors most often associated with the Tiger tank – and with considerable justification – are but two of the major elements

Above: A tank of *1.Kp/s.Pz.Abt. 501*'s 4th Platoon in Bizerte, January, 1943. Here, it is running on transport tracks, with its outer roadwheels detached, having travelled to Sicily initially by rail. This failure to switch to combat tracks when on the road caused huge logistical problems for Tiger units later in the war.

which influence a tank's survivability. Manoeuvrability and mechanical reliability count for almost as much, but a further factor needs to be taken into consideration, too – what we today call ergonomics. This affects not just the design of the fighting compartment and accommodation, with all that implies for the efficiency of the crew, but also the factor of accessibility for routine maintenance and major repair. As far as the designer is concerned, developing a concept for a new tank is a fairly complex process, within which all those factors must be balanced and coordinated.

DESIGNERS' PROBLEMS

Presented with the most basic requirements – perhaps no more than the protection characteristics and the level of armament necessary to defeat a particular enemy tank – the designer constructs a notional framework into which he slots the other ingredients, juggling them until he arrives at a workable mix and making the inevitable trade-offs along the way. He is constrained all along by 'artificial' components outside his control, such as the maximum loading gauge of the railway system which the vehicle would have to utilise, the weight limit of roads and railway bridges and the physical size and form of available weapons and powerplants.

He adds to these such esoteric requirements as the need to maintain the ratio between the length of track in contact with the ground and the distance between the tracks as close to the unitary as possible, since the higher that ratio is allowed to go, the more difficult a tank becomes to steer. All the above, and many other, elements must be taken into consideration – facility (or at least, practicality) of manufac-

ture and raw materials requirements not least among them. But, above all, the tank designer is ultimately charged with producing a design for a vehicle capable of winning the battle to which it will be committed. In the armoured battle, perhaps more than in any other form of land fighting, tactics, skill and training often count for less than the physical ability of the opposing vehicles to give and take punishment, and the designer, who will probably never fight in the vehicle himself, thus plays an all-important role.

DESIGN SOLUTIONS

It is fair to say that the Tiger tank's designers played their parts wholeheartedly, though there were areas where their work fell short of expectations. Some of the errors they made might have been avoided, but most were forced on them – the result of the short time available for development. (Though for a better idea of the potential for mistakes under such circumstances, one only has to look at the Panther tank development programme.) Nevertheless, considering that the first production models of the new tank were delivered in little more than nine months from the project's official commencment, the result was quite remarkable.

One of the designer's most important assets is the ability to adapt shape and form to optimise the performance of his creation and to compensate for factors outside his control.

PzKpfw VI Tiger (SdKfz 181) Ausf E

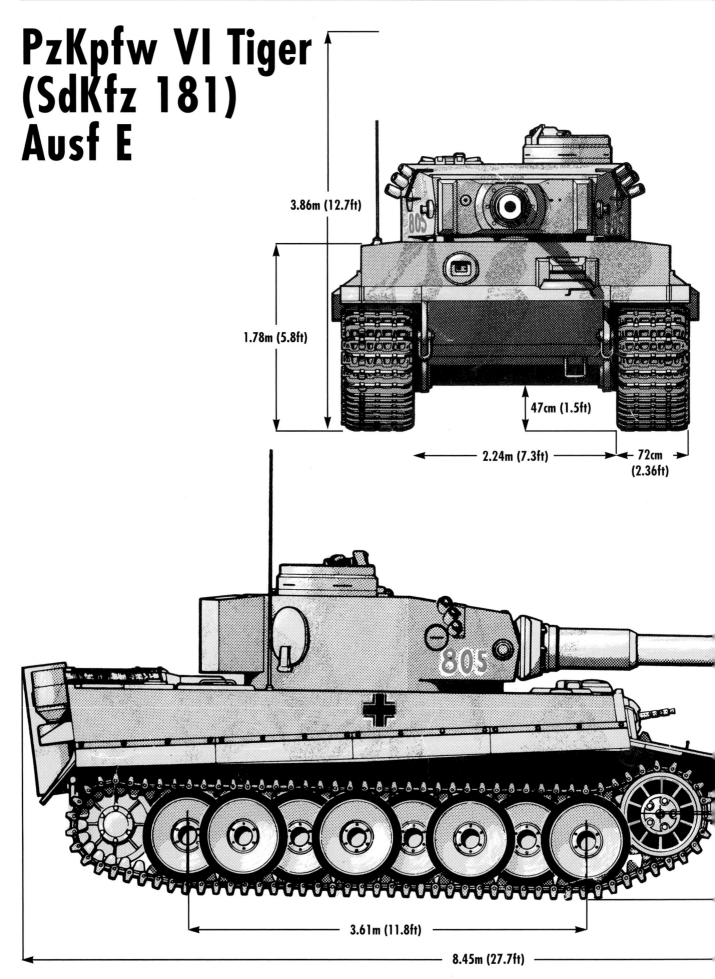

3.86m (12.7ft)

1.78m (5.8ft)

47cm (1.5ft)

2.24m (7.3ft)

72cm (2.36ft)

3.61m (11.8ft)

8.45m (27.7ft)

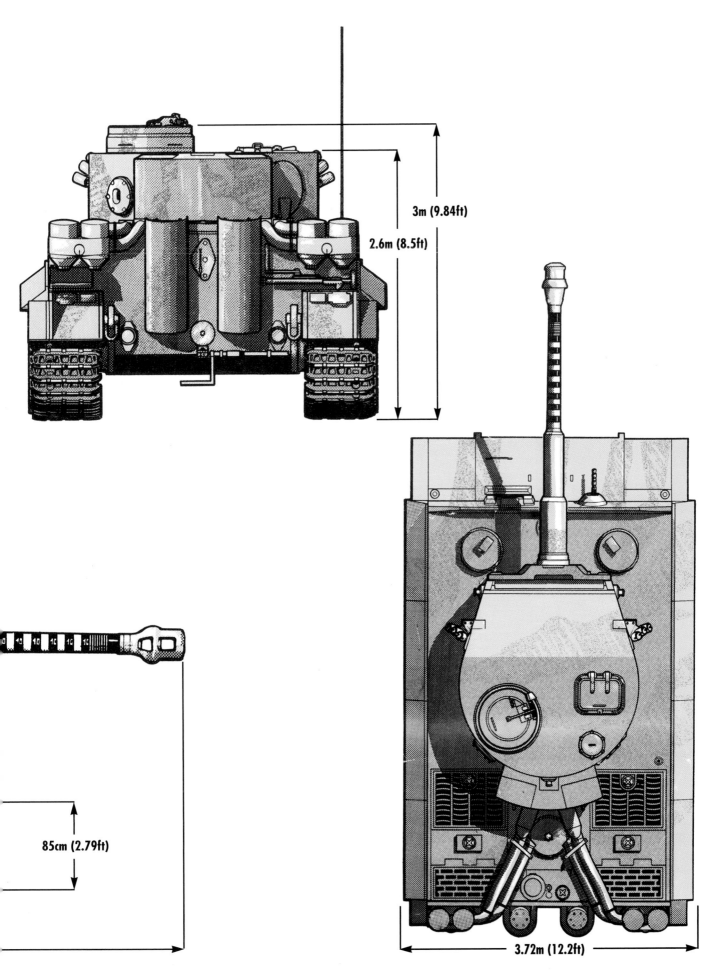

3m (9.84ft)

2.6m (8.5ft)

85cm (2.79ft)

3.72m (12.2ft)

One of the tank designer's chief concerns is to provide as much protection as possible within a given weight budget, and in this task there is only a very limited amount of reshaping and re-forming he can do. Short of redefining the composition of the armour itself (an option which was largely unavailable in 1942), the most straightforward method is to set the protective armour at an angle, thus both increasing its effective thickness 'head-on' and giving it a pronounced tendency to deflect incoming shot. During the 1920s and 1930s there was some argument as to how effective this ploy was; tanks were likely to meet each other at widely differing angles, it was suggested, and thus little benefit would derive from the angling of armour plate.

That argument may have had some validity when the tank's prime function was to support the infantry in storming fixed defensive positions, where trenches and other obstacles often forced them into extreme attitudes, but by 1941 this was no longer the case. Tank-versus-tank battles were now the norm; they were being fought in open country, where opposing tanks were at or close to zero angle relative to each other, and angled armour had proved its effectiveness over and over again.

However, in the design and specification of the Tiger tank, very little attempt was made to employ armour at an angle, in either the vertical or the horizontal plane. This factor, above all others, defines the essential character of the Tiger, and also, perhaps, betrays both the haste with which its form was defined and the undeniable fact that it was essentially

Above: Heinz Guderian, *Generalinspekteur der Panzertruppen*, with ultimate responsibility for all Germany's tank forces, took a personal interest in anything to do with Tigers. Here, he inspects a tank of *schwere Kompanie/ SS-Pz. Rgt 2*, which formed part of the 2nd SS Panzer Divsion, *Das Reich*.

transitional. A comparison of the Tiger with the earlier, much smaller, PzKpfw III and IV, reveals a distinct similarity in this respect. The similarity had its advantages: Allied, particularly American soldiers, it is said, frequently mistook PzKpfw IVs for Tigers, and adjusted their behaviour accordingly. On the other hand a comparison with the two successor tanks, the Panther, which also appeared in 1942, and the King Tiger, design studies for which started that year, show that German designers' ideas soon fell in line with those of their enemies.

ANGLED ARMOUR

It is difficult to understand why Henschel's designers came up with what is essentially a square box for the Tiger's hull. Sloped armour had been incorporated into earlier German designs: the *Grosstraktor* and even more particularly the *Leichttraktor* of the late 1920s incorporated long, sloping frontal glacis plates, and so did the diminutive PzKpfw I. But in the Tiger, this vital component is set almost vertically. Difficulties of fabrication – though not of forming, since the sides and rear of the turret of the Henschel Tigers, for example, were a single piece of 80mm- (3.15in-) thick homogeneous armour, bent into a horseshoe shape with a radius of only a little over 1m (3.3ft) – are sometimes cited, though the Tiger's all-welded construction would certainly have permitted sloping armour. The same was not true of the PzKpfw III and IV, where armour sub-assemblies were prefabricated and then bolted together. Perhaps the form of these vehicles somehow influenced the Tiger's designers.

The only steeply sloping element on the Tiger was the short glacis plate, forward of the hull upper front plate with its ball-mounted machine gun and driver's vision slots, which was set at 81 degrees to the vertical. In the event, the vertical plating was massive enough to withstand virtually anything. But if its hull and turret armour had been placed at a significant angle to the vertical wherever possible, the Tiger would have been a still better tank, because it would have been possible to reduce its all-up weight, which was always a major concern. For example, if the front plate had been set at an angle of 35 degrees, 60mm- (2.4in-) thick plate would have given the same level of protection, head-on and at zero relative angle, as the near vertical 100mm (4in) plate. Had this exercise been carried out wherever possible, a significant weight saving would have resulted.

THE TIGER'S ARMOUR

The armour standard for the Tiger was massive, by any comparison. The exposed vertical and near vertical faces – the upper and lower plate, the turret sides and the hull sides and rear, which was not vertical, but set at 81 degrees, parallel with the front plate – were to be a maximum 100mm (4in) and a minimum 80mm (3.15in) thick. The short, steeply angled front glacis plate and the lower hull side plates, inboard of the roadwheels, were 60mm (2.4in) thick – the large-diameter interlocking wheels themselves provided added protection – while the most vulnerable area of all, the face of the turret, was to be 120mm (4.7in) thick, and was further reinforced over much of its area by a cast-steel mantlet of similar thickness attached to the base of the gun tube. This specification meant, essentially, that the Tiger's hull and turret were virtually impervious to the T-34's 76mm gun at any range greater than 300–400m (330–440yds), no matter from what angle the attack came.

The horizontal and near-horizontal faces – the turret top and the hull top, including the engine cover, as well as the belly of the tank – were more lightly protected, but still to 25mm (1in) thickness. In general, the level of protection here was considered adequate, though there were numerous incidents of tanks being lost to plunging artillery fire which pierced their top armour, and there were even occasions when the light tanks and armoured cars, which could never have taken on a Tiger in a conventional encounter, succeeded in knocking out one of the monsters by manoeuvring so as to be able to get in a shot from above or into the rear plate from a very close range.

The vulnerability of the rear plate was compounded by its being cluttered with engine exhaust covers, air filters and the like, which acted as shot traps.

When close-support fighter–bomber aircraft came into wider use, particularly in 1944 and 1945, the vulnerability of the turret- and hull-top armour proved the Tiger's undoing. Rocket-armed aircraft, such as the RAF's Hawker

Typhoons and Tempests were the most successful against them, and were probably the single biggest destroyer of Tigers in the field. But cannon- and bomb-armed P-47 Thunderbolts and P-51 Mustangs and the Soviet Air Force's Il-2 and Il-10 Stormoviks were also devastatingly effective. The decision to use such relatively light-gauge plate on the Tiger's upper surfaces was an atypical failure to foresee a future trend. At no time was the armour over the engine increased in thickness, but from mid-1944 the thickness of the turret top was increased to 40 or 45mm (1.57 or 1.77in).

German manufacturers did not introduce flame-cutting techniques for armour plate until 1944, using oxy-acetylene at first, and oxy-propane later, and so all Tiger tank armour was cut to shape mechanically, using tungsten-tipped tools.

Apart from the weight and thickness of the armour plate, the sheer size of the Tiger created problems of dimensional stability and rigidity. In an attempt to overcome them, plates of the largest possible size were used. The belly plate, for example, was cut from a single piece of 25mm (1in) homogeneous steel, almost 5m (16ft) long and 1.8m (6ft) wide. Considerable attention was paid to the integrity of welded

Above: An *s.Pz.Abt. 508* Tiger tank in Rome on 20 February 1944 makes its way south to the Anzio beachhead, in an attempt to prevent the Allies breaking out. Tanks tend to collect both hitchhikers and other non-regulation additions when out of the frontline – this one has managed to acquire a motorcycle!

joints, too, both for the effect this had on the rigidity of the structure as a whole and in order to optimise resistance to incoming fire. The edges to be joined were both stepped and cut so as to interlock, much in the manner of a woodworker's cross-halving or mortise-and-tenon joint. The best examples of this technique are seen not in the Tiger but in the PzKpfw V Panther, and are particularly obvious where the sloping upper and lower glacis plates meet. The technique, which produces less stress in the joints than in simple juxtaposed welds, seems to have been used originally in the construction of heavy machinery such as presses.

A process of austenitic electro-arc welding was used throughout. This both completed the joint in a single pass, where previously three passes had been required, and also produced a truly homogeneous union. It even allowed armour plating to be joined to cast armour without any loss of strength, though this was not employed on the Tiger. Although reports on captured tanks by British and American engineers criticised both the quality of the added metal (from the electrode) and the workmanship, the structural integrity of the welding on the tanks' hulls was widely praised – a sure indicator that the designers had envisaged problems occurring during production and had devised a way to overcome them at the specification stage.

Machinable homogeneous armour (that is, plate of a consistent quality throughout, rather than plate which had been face-hardened, usually by means of carburizing) was used

Below: The Tiger's upper and rear surfaces were highly vulnerable to enemy fire. The armour plate on the turret and hull tops was originally only 25mm (1in) thick, and could be penetrated by even small-calibre anti-tank weapons.

exclusively. Spaced supplemental armour, which showed up on later models of both the PzKpfw III and IV, was never employed on Tiger tanks, although armoured skirts (*Schürzen*) were occasionally fitted to protect the tracks, particularly against attack from rocket-propelled grenades and satchel charges in the hands of assault pioneers.

THE CHOICE OF GUN

It is popularly supposed that Adolf Hitler himself insisted that the 8.8cm L/56 gun was to equip the Tiger tank, in place of the improved and lengthened version of the 7.5cm gun which had been originally specified and under development at Rheinmetall since July 1941. This gun, which was designated the KwK 42 when it was later fitted to the PzKpfw V Panther, had a barrel 70 calibres long, and hence an overall length of 5.25m (17ft), 32cm (12.5in) longer than the KwK 36. Its 6.8kg (15lb) APCBC Pzgr.39 round could penetrate 110mm (4.4in) of armour at 30 degrees at 1000m (1090yds), while the 4.75kg (10.5lb) tungsten-cored Pzgr.40 7.5cm round could penetrate 150mm (5.9in). This contrasts very favourably with the 100mm (4in) and 138mm (5.45in) penetration the same ammunition types in 8.8cm calibre achieved from the KwK 36. The difference is the result of the longer barrel allowing the projectile to be accelerated for longer, thus achieving a considerably higher muzzle velocity – 925m/sec (3035ft/sec) and 1120m/sec (4265ft/sec) for the 7.5cm round, 773m/sec (2536ft/sec) and 930m/sec (3015ft/sec) for the 8.8cm – the increased velocity making up for the reduced mass. The further advantage of the smaller-calibre gun lies in the lighter weight and smaller size of each round of ammunition; lighter rounds are

easier to handle, particularly in the confined space of a tank's hull and turret, while smaller rounds naturally take up less stowage space. It was ready to go into production in June 1942, and thus would have been available for the first Tigers, which came off the production lines themselves two months later.

THE DETERMINING FACTOR

Yet despite these potential advantages, it was the bigger-calibre gun which found its way into the Tiger, with all that meant for the eventual overall size of the resultant tank. Was the 8.8cm gun essential to the Tiger's success? A tank with the same level of protection as the Tiger but armed with the smaller gun would inevitably have been lighter, since the size of the gun, by dictating the size of the turret in which it is mounted, eventually decides the size of the vehicle which will carry it. The tank in question might conceivably even have stayed within the fairly arbitrary 45-tonne (44.3-ton) legend weight, or at least have come closer to it than the 56 tonnes (55 tons) at which the Tiger rolled out. Certainly, it would have been hardly less effective in offensive terms than the Tiger as it emerged in late 1942, while a substantial reduction in weight would have gone a long way towards alleviating the operational problems inherent in the overweight tank. The choice of the KwK 36 over the KwK 42 was therefore crucial.

Above: The vulnerability of the Tiger's rear plate was compounded by its being cluttered with engine exhaust covers, air filters and the like, which acted as shot traps.

It is sometimes argued that the 45-tonne (44.3-ton) design was favoured over the 30- and 36-tonne (29.5- and 35.5-ton) tanks just because it could accept the 8.8cm gun 'and in doing so secure an advantage in firepower', as one expert has put it – but that advantage was illusory. It did not matter whether it was a 7.5cm round or an 8.8cm round that penetrated the enemy tank, since penetration with either meant an almost certain kill, particularly with a Pzgr.39 round, which had a high-explosive filling. In any event, whether it was Hitler himself or the Tank Development Commission (*Entwicklungskommission Panzer*) that decided which gun was to be used, the guiding principle was clearly to take no chances.

The KwK 36 evolved from an anti-aircraft gun, originally developed in the days before the Nazis came to power in a secret joint venture between Krupp and the Swedish armaments manufacturer, Bofors. This gun, the FlaK 18, went into service in 1933, and established the 8.8cm calibre (which had been first introduced during World War I). Its one major weakness was its short barrel life – just 900 rounds to begin with, though this was later increased to 3000 when the propellant charge was changed. This was

Above: Out of the battle line, the Tiger always needed a great deal of repair work to bring it back up to scratch. Here, a maintenance team from 2nd SS Panzer Division *Das Reich*'s *s.SS-Pz. Abt. 502* works on one of its tanks, probably, as the tank is painted in light tan, prior to Operation *Zitadelle*.

still considered to be inadequate, particularly since the gun was capable of sustaining a firing rate of 15 rounds per minute. Rheinmetall, Krupp's main rival, was told to come up with a solution. The answer was a three-part liner, which was simpler and cheaper to change than the entire barrel, and the gun thus modified entered service as the FlaK 18/36.

During the Spanish Civil War, in the latter half of the 1930s, the 8.8cm FlaK was occasionally used in the anti-

tank role. By 1940 this had become accepted practice, and all AAA units were routinely provided with armour-piercing ammunition (*Panzergranate*). So successful were these expedient anti-tank weapons that they became an established part of the tactical order of battle, used at long range to screen armoured formations. After the invasion of the Soviet Union in the summer of 1941, when the PzKpfw III and IVs in both army and SS panzer divisions were found to be vulnerable to the 76mm L/41 high-velocity guns in the Russian T-34 and KV-1 tanks at long range, the towed 8.8cm guns proved to be the only viable anti-tank weapon they had. It was the experience of Operation 'Barbarossa' that prompted the cancellation of the 30-tonne (29.5-ton)

tank development programme and the commissioning of the Tiger programme in its place. It is not surprising, therefore, that a version of the trusted, reliable 8.8cm gun was specified for the new vehicle.

FIRE BY WIRE

The 8.8cm gun as fitted to the Tiger differed slightly from the versions used as anti-aircraft guns. It was fired electrically, using heat generated by a charge passing across a resistance (essentially, nothing more complicated than a length of fuse wire) within the propellant charge, rather than by percussion, the action of a firing pin on a primer 'cap' containing fulminate of mercury. Thus, though the ammunition for the two guns was dimensionally identical, it was not interchangeable. However, to eliminate any gross logistical problems, 8.8cm towed anti-tank guns, which could be expected to operate alongside the tanks, were equipped with the same electrical system, and so used the same ammunition as the Tigers. The Tiger's gun was fitted with a modified double-baffle muzzle brake, which redirected some of the propellant

Above: Judging by the lack of a hull machine gun and mudguards, and the absence of a tactical number, this Tiger is probably a refurbished tank allocated to a training unit after undergoing major repair at Henschel's Kassel factory. These tanks were returned to service during the last months of the war.

gases, and thus both lessened the recoil, by as much as 70 per cent, and churned up less dust and debris in dry conditions – an important consideration, since the gunner's view was easily obscured. The gun could not be fired without the muzzle brake – or, at least, not more than once.

The most accurate and powerful gun is only as good as its sighting and aiming system, and here the Germans had a traditional advantage over their enemies, since their optical industry was the best in the world at that time. The Tiger was fitted with an articulated binocular turret gunsight (*Turmzielfernrohr* – TZF), its twin objectives fixed parallel to the main gun tube. The TZF 9b, in use up until April 1944, had a fixed 2.5x magnification, while the TZF 9c in use thereafter offered either 2.5x or 5x magnification. Apart from that they were essentially similar. Each tube of the sight had

a different illuminated reticle pattern. The left tube carried the graticules or aiming point marks – a central triangle with three subsidiary points to each side, which allowed both for leading a moving target and to assist with estimating range. The right tube had the aiming point marks but also range scales, arranged in arcs to right and left, for the main gun and the coaxial machine gun respectively, the former graduating out to 4000m (4400yds), the latter to 1200m (1310yds).

STADIAMETRIC RANGEFINDING

These range scales were in the form of *aides-mèmoire*, and could be rotated so that the estimated range coincided with an indexing mark. There was no device within the sight to assist with rangefinding that was more sophisticated than the set of subsidiary aiming points. Stadiametric range determination, as the technique is known, was the norm for the period, and was based on experience: the gunner was expected to know how far a target's image would extend across the scale at any given range. More precise ranging was derived from bracketing – the gunner would fire a round, and then compensate by increasing or decreasing the elevation of the gun as necessary before firing again. This was not as approximative a process as one might imagine, thanks to the flat trajectory of the 8.8cm gun.

A trained gunner was expected to be able to hit a stationary target at 1200m (1310yds) with his first round, and bracketing was only necessary at greater distances to the maximum effective combat range of 2000m (2250yds). At that range, he was expected to be on target by the fourth round. Against a moving target travelling at 20kmph

Above: Shown here negotiating a steep bank in soft going during acceptance trials, this very early production Tiger (it lacks the 'cyclone' air cleaners invented by Prof. Feifel of the Vienna Technische Hochschule in 1943) has yet to be allocated to a combat unit, hence its lack of distinguishing markings.

(12.5mph) across his front, at a range of 800–1200m (875–1310yds), the gunner was expected to be able to score a hit within three rounds, and within 30 seconds each.

COINCIDENCE RANGEFINDERS

Optical coincidence rangefinders were issued to Tiger tanks, but they could only be used externally, located in a bracket attached to the commander's cupola in later tanks but hand-held in the earliest models. Essentially they were low-power binoculars with a narrow field of view, arranged so that the ray path to each eyepiece was derived from objectives 1m (3.3ft) or more apart – the TZR 1 unit issued to Tiger tanks from quite early in 1943 had a base measurement of 1.4m (4.6ft). The range to the target was read off a scale, as the angle between the two objective lenses was adjusted until the images at the eyepiece coincided.

The gunner laid the gun on its target by elevating it within the turret and traversing – turning the turret – in combination. Elevation – from minus 6.5 degrees to plus 17 degrees – was carried out manually, by means of a 190mm- (7.5in-) diameter handwheel mounted on a horizontal shaft, operated by the gunner's right hand. The 'trigger' to fire the main gun was located on the elevating gear shaft, close to the wheel. It could be actuated with one finger.

The Tiger was equipped with hydraulic turret traverse, the pump which powered it being driven off the main gearbox through a small auxiliary. The system performed one complete revolution of the turret in a minimum of about 25 and a maximum of 60 seconds, depending on the speed at which the engine was turning over. (By way of comparison, an M4 Sherman's power traverse could turn the turret through 360 degrees in 10 seconds. This advantage was often cited as being decisive.) It was used to bring the gun to bear in the general direction of the target, to somewhere within the 23-degree field-of-view of the TZF 9 sight, whereupon the gunner switched to hand traverse to point it accurately, at a rate of two turns of a 260mm- (10.25in-) diameter handwheel per degree of traverse. The commander was provided with a traversing handwheel, too, which was higher-geared than the gunner's and slaved to it in a sense, since the gunner's traversing wheel incorporated a lock which only he could release; the commander had no access to the power traverse control. Both had simple clock-like indicators to show the position of the turret relative to the fore-and-aft axis of the tank, and the gunner was also provided with a clinometer to indicate the gun's elevation. The manual traverse could be used in case the hydraulics failed, or when the main engine was not in use, but a long traverse by hand was a tedious business. The hydraulic mechanism was not particularly precise, and the poor placement and design of the foot pedal which when actuated did nothing to improve its usability. (It had no automatic return to the null or neutral position, and this must have been a constant source of overcompensation.)

A 'motion study' report on what we would now call the tank's ergonomics, prepared by a British officer in 1947, singles out the gunner's position for considerable criticism, both in its general arrangements and in the layout of the gun controls. The report concluded: 'In general, the gunner's position is very bad. It is very cramped, the gun controls are badly designed and positioned, and the vision facilities are inadequate.' It criticised the bow gunner's, the commander's, and the driver's positions, too, and suggested that only the loader could have been at all comfortable. We shall return to that report at greater length in due course.

AMMUNITION STOWAGE

The Tiger was provided with stowage space for 92 rounds of 8.8cm ammunition, in 10 bins, each holding 16, six or four rounds, depending on where they were placed. All bins held their rounds horizontally, fore-and-aft. The ready ammunition – 64 rounds – was held in four bins in the hull sides; 16 more rounds were held in four bins in the hull floor, whch were also accessible to the loader, but far less easily than those in the hull sides. The last 12 rounds, which were generally used only to replenish the ready ammunition bins, were located six beside the driver's position and six below the turret turntable. The latter were not available while the tank

Below: The flimsy looking gantry crane supplied to each Tiger battalion's Workshop Company was in fact designed to be as light as possible while still performing specialised tasks, such as replacing turret assemblies, a necessary prerequisite to changing a transmission – unfortunately a common task.

Above: The ammunition loading hatch in the rear of the Krupp-designed turret of the King Tiger was a useful secondary access to the interior and could be closed from within. In the later tank, spent cases could be thrown out this way, while on the Tiger they had to be thrown clear via the loader's roof hatch.

was in action, but the six rounds stored next to the driver were accessible with the gun in the straight-ahead position. With the ready ammunition bins full, there were never less than 20 rounds available to the loader, no matter what the position of the turret relative to the hull. Loading was a straightforward process to begin with, but became increasingly difficult as ammunition was expended, and the loader had to reach further into the bins to find fresh rounds, a process that was impeded by the design of the cradles in which each round lay. It is worth bearing in mind that a Pzgr.39 round weighed something in excess of 16kg (35.3lb). The British motion study found that the average loading time for the main gun was 6.4 seconds, and the reporting officer regarded that as 'unnecessarily high'.

MACHINE GUNS

Tiger tanks were also fitted in the field with two and sometimes four extra racks, each holding seven rounds, located above the main pannier bins, which increased the modified tanks' ammunition capacity to 106 or 120 rounds. It is unclear whether this modification was made at battalion level, or whether it was carried out on instructions from Germany. The preferred mix of armour-piercing and high-

Left: The drop-down hatch in the right-rear of the Tiger's turret (which appeared halfway through 1943) was designed for loading main gun ammunition, though it could be used as an escape hatch. However, it was impossible to close from the inside, and once opened, obstructed the turret's traverse.

explosive rounds was half and half. The tungsten-cored Pzgr.40 rounds were always in very short supply, and when they were issued – at a rate of between four and six to a tank – they were supposed to be held in reserve for particularly difficult targets.

SECONDARY ARMAMENT

The Tiger tank's secondary armament consisted of two MG34 general-purpose 7.92mm machine guns. Developed in the early 1930s by Rheinmetall, using a method of locking the bolt devised by Mauser, the MG34 was by far the most complex and complicated machine gun at the time, but it was also, undoubtedly, the best. All that was required to convert the gun from a bipod or tripod mount, as employed by the infantry, to a flexible vehicle mount was to slide it into the ball mount and push in a locating pin. The butt-stock was simply detached, leaving the pistol grip in place. The MG34 could be fed from a complex double-drum magazine holding 75 rounds, but this was too bulky for use inside an armoured vehicle, and the alternative belt-feed system was always employed. Ammunition was stored in bags adjacent to the two gun installations, 150 rounds per bag. A full load comprised a total of 34 belts – 5100 rounds

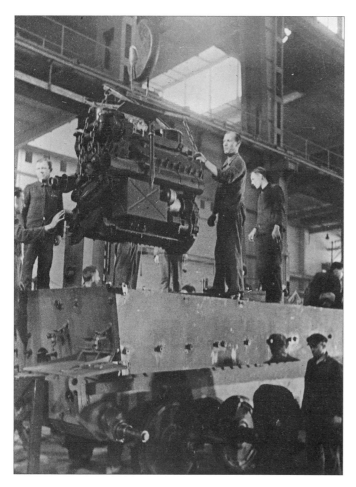

Above: Thanks to careful design, both the installation of the Tiger's Maybach powerplant (the HL210 unit with its 21-l engine shown here and later superseded by the larger-capacity HL230) and its replacement in the field were relatively easy tasks, even though the engines weighed close to three-quarters of a tonne.

in all. On later models of the Tiger, fitted with the cupola designed for the Panther, a third machine gun could be mounted on a simple pintle at the commander's hatch, for use against aircraft or, more effectively, targets on the ground.

THE MACHINE GUNNER

The bow machine gun, located in a ball mount in the front plate, on the nearside of the tank, was directed and controlled by the pistol grip and by a padded headpan which was linked to the mount, and fired by an ordinary finger-operated trigger. It could be depressed and elevated through 30 degrees (minus 10 degrees to plus 20 degrees) and traversed through a similar arc, 15 degrees to left or right. The ball mount was located quite some way down the barrel cover towards the muzzle, which afforded limited independent movement and meant that the gun was distinctly out of balance and breech-heavy – an 'equilibrator' or compensating spring did not entirely correct matters. The report quoted earlier says, 'the headpan pressed down heavily on the bow gunner's head *causing acute discomfort*' (italics in original).

The bow gunner was provided with a standard KZF 2 sighting telescope with 1.8x magnification and an 18-degree field of view, fixed to the gun and moving with it;

this was the only means he had of searching for targets independently. His gun was easily loaded and stripped for maintenance, in contrast to the coaxially mounted gun in the turret, which was notoriously difficult to replenish and not easy to demount. The latter, which was loaded and maintained by the main gun loader, was fired by the main gunner by means of a foot pedal. Unfortunately, this was located too close to the power-traverse pedal, and in firing the machine gun the gunner was likely inadvertently to set the turret in motion too. Where an 'anti-aircraft' machine gun was mounted, though such a weapon would have been next to useless against air attack and was much more likely to have been employed against troops and soft-skinned targets on the ground, it could have been an MG34 or its successor, the essentially similar MG42. No special anti-aircraft sights were fitted.

In addition, one 9mm MP40 machine pistol was carried inside the vehicle, and many crew members carried 9mm P38 or occasionally P08 pistols. Anti-personnel hand grenades, which could be thrown out through the pistol ports in the turret (two in early Tigers, one in later models), were also carried. There were three launchers for 92mm bombs or grenades mounted on the turret top and accessible from within the vehicle, though these were deleted from new vehicles sometime in mid-1944, and were removed from existing vehicles as and when they went for major overhaul. Six smoke generators were mounted, three on each side of the turret, at the front. These were also removed, following an incident in which a tank was lost when a smoke generator was set off by small-arms fire, incapacitating the crew.

MAYBACH ENGINES

The diminutive PzKp LaS A, the first of the panzers to go into service, in 1934, was the last German tank of World War II to be powered by anything but a Maybach engine. This *de facto* monopoly, which extended also to artillery prime movers, gave the Friedrichshafen company and its founder and head, Dr Karl Maybach, an unprecedented clear run at developing appropriate powerplants. By the end of the war, the company had delivered roughly 140,000 engines of various types (50,000 of them HL210/230s and derivatives), as well as thousands of semi-automatic gearboxes, such as the OLVAR transmission specified for the Tiger. Only in the Soviet Union was there a comparable system of standardisation of tank powerplants. Neither Britain nor the United States ever achieved anything like this degree of coordination. The M4 Sherman tank, for example, was powered by no less than five very different engines from five different manufacturers – a logistical nightmare in the field. Only one of those powerplants – the 18l, 500hp Ford GAA V-8 – was actually developed for the purpose; all the others were derived from engines conceived for other applications, including aircraft.

The engine originally specified for the Tiger was a liquid-cooled 60-degree V-12 unit of 21 litres nominal capacity, with a single overhead camshaft per cylinder bank and four twin-choke, down-draught Solex carburettors. It delivered 642hp at 3000rpm, to which maximum speed it was governed. This powerplant – the HL210 P45 – was fitted to the

Above: To keep the Tiger's profile as low as possible, the turret height was kept down, so the main armament could not be depressed more than 6.5 degrees below the horizontal before the breech hit the turret roof. This undamaged Tiger has been abandoned, perhaps due to transmission failure.

first 250 production Tigers, and was then superseded by the 23l HL230 P45, which produced 52hp more. Probably the most remarkable thing about the HL210/230 engines was their physical size. They were hardly longer overall than the HL120 series from which they were derived, but, as their designation suggests, were of almost twice the capacity and were more than twice as powerful. The bigger-capacity HL230 was actually almost 10 per cent shorter still than the HL210, thanks to a more intelligent means of mounting certain ancillaries. In comparison, a Bedford V-8 engine of similar capacity (21.3l) powered the 40-tonne (39.4-ton) Churchill tank; it gave just 325hp.

A better comparison is perhaps to be made between the HL230 and the Rolls-Royce Meteor engine, which was fitted to the A27(M) Cromwell, the A34 Comet and the A41 Centurion. The Meteor was a normally aspirated (that is, unsupercharged) version of the 27l Merlin aero engine. First produced in 1936, it was an advanced design, with twin exhaust and inlet valves and twin spark plugs, but was essentially similar in character to the HL230, being a 60-degree V-12 with a single overhead camshaft per bank of cylinders, though it had nondetachable cylinder heads. It, too, was a wet-liner design, but with a conventional crankshaft. It weighed some 750kg (1653lb) and produced 600hp at 2500rpm – a severely down-rated performance from that of

the engine from which it was derived, which by 1943 was producing over 1600hp. Its power/weight ratio of 0.8hp/kg (0.36hp/lb) compared very favourably with the HL230's 0.6hp/kg (0.26hp/lb). In the 28-tonne (27.5-ton) Cromwell it consumed 9-12l (1.98 UK gallons/2.4 US gallons-2.64 UK gallons/3.2 US gallons) of fuel per mile cross-country and about half that on the road, and gave the tank a maximum road speed of well over 60kmph (37.3mph).

The 300hp HL120 was a tried and tested unit, having been used in both the PzKpfw III and IV, but the bigger powerplant was much more than simply a scaling-up. The crankshaft, for example, was of a completely different design, being made up of a series of seven disks, mounted in large-diameter main bearings and linked by the crankshaft pins supporting paired connecting rods. (It was this innovation that permitted the massive overall reduction in length. One of the pair of connecting rods was conventional, the other had two rather narrower bearing surfaces, and was in the form of a yoke; the former was mounted within the latter.) The use of wet cylinder liners meant that cooling was

unaffected, even though the cylinders were barely a millimetre apart across the engine's longitudinal axis. The HL230 powerplant weighed 1200kg (2646lb) with an aluminium cylinder block and cast-iron heads; an all-aluminium unit was tested, but never went into production.

While the engines – and particularly the HL230 – were excellent, they were not perfect and especially not within the context of an already-heavy tank which came out at 25 per cent over its specified weight. In particular, the engines had a disturbing tendency to allow coolant into the oilways if their operating temperature exceeded 95 degrees C (203 degrees F); this seems to have been due to the nature of the synthetic rubber used in the sealing rings, and not a design defect, however, and other engines also exhibited the same tendency. This was not the only basic flaw in German hardware caused by shortages of strategic materials.

SPEED AND POWERPLANT

Rushed into production before the development process was entirely complete, early models were prone to breakdowns, but more crucial than the failures occasioned by insufficient testing was the fact that more was expected of them than they could reasonably give. A power/weight ratio of 12.35hp/tonne is no recipe for sparkling performance, and leaves little margin for error. Thanks to the relatively high final drive ratio permitted by the eight-speed transmission, the top speed of the Tiger on the road was a fairly reasonable 37kmph (23mph). (This is 10kmph [6.2mph] less than the T-34, with its power/weight ratio of 19hp/tonne which, we

Above: Each of the 96 links in a Tiger's combat tracks weighed 30kg (66lb), so each complete track weighed 2.88 tonnes (2.82 tons). Since the tracks had to be changed each time the tanks were loaded on a train, this was a major problem, and required both considerable manpower and special techniques.

may recall, the Tiger outweighed by a factor of two, and 3–4kmph (1.9–2.5mph) slower than the M4 Sherman.) But across country the Tiger's effective top speed dropped to around a half of that.

The same powerplant, in slightly modified form as the P30, was specified for the 45-tonne (44.3-ton) Panther, where it performed rather better, if, initially, no more reliably. (This was the original design weight for the Tiger; the power/weight ratio being a more realistic, though still not generous, 15.4hp/tonne.) It was also specified for the 70-tonne (68.9-ton) King Tiger, where it was even more heavily overstretched, particularly after being downrated to 600hp in an attempt to improve reliability. The result of the powerplant being overstretched, not surprisingly, was a low mean time between failures. On the credit side, however, the engine could be removed and replaced remarkably quickly, since access to it was very good in all three vehicles.

In simple terms, the high all-up weight of the Tiger meant that the engine was always required to deliver a high percentage of its available power. That, combined with the fact that Tigers were so much in demand that routine maintenance was often skimped, was the main contributory factor to its unreliability, particularly when a tank was further overstrained by being used to tow others. But more important, it had a massive effect on fuel consumption. Captured German tankers astounded the Allied soldiers who took them prisoner, telling them that the Tiger's full fuel load of 567 litres (125 UK gal/156.25 US gal) rarely lasted more than two and a half hours when operating off-road. The 'official' figure was 7.8 l/km (2.75 UK gal/3.45 US gal/mile) in 'normal' cross-country running, though reports reveal that a true consumption of 10 l/km was more realistic, when running-up and traversing the turret while stationary were taken into account. This was undoubtedly the Tiger tank's biggest operational failing.

AN EXCELLENT GEARBOX

The engine was installed in the rear of the tank, driving forwards via a propellor shaft located beneath the turret floor and above the suspension torsion bars, which occupied most of the space in the very bottom of the hull, to the gearbox, which incorporated the hydraulically actuated three-plate clutch. The steering unit was bolted directly to the front of the gearbox, and drove the tracks via a final reduction gear in the hub of each drive sprocket. The gearbox itself – Maybach's OLVAR – was the most complex and expensive component of the Tiger tank. A pre-selector unit, which provided eight forward speeds and four in reverse from four constantly meshed gear sets and a transfer set, the OLVAR gearbox was hydraulically actuated. Its ease of operation was in direct (and probably proportional) contrast to its complexity of design and manufacture, but Tiger tank drivers were unanimous in their praise for it.

The steering unit was regenerative, with an epicyclic train to each sprocket, driven from both the input to and the output from the main gearbox. Essentially, the steering unit separated the power train into two components; the main drive functioned as normal, but the subsidiary drive, which took its power off the input shaft to the gearbox, could be directed to one or other of the tracks to supplement it, thereby inducing one track to turn faster than the other, and thus slew the tank to left or right. With the main drive in neutral, only the supplementary drive functioned, and at 'full lock', drove one track in one direction and the other in the reverse, thus enabling the tank to turn in its own length.

This system had been pioneered in the UK and had first been employed in the Churchill tank; the German version

Below: Each of the Tiger's tracks ran on eight sets of three 800mm- (31.5in-) diameter roadwheels. The wheels were extra protection for the lower part of the hull, and its armour plating was reduced as a result. The multi-wheel arrangement gave an even ride, but mud and debris between the disks remained a major problem.

Above: The inside of a *Sturmtiger*, which had a built-up superstructure to accommodate a 38cm assault mortar. Its seven-man crew was just as cramped as their counterparts serving in Tiger 1s.

was produced after captured vehicles had been studied. Both the speed and the direction of turn were controlled hydraulically from a conventional steering wheel. This was the first time a regenerative steering system had been installed in a German tank, which up until then had relied on much simpler, but less efficient, differential or clutch/brake systems. Like the OLVAR transmission, it was universally popular with Tiger crews. Disk brakes on the final driveshafts between the steering unit and the drive sprockets also functioned as emergency steering brakes, and could be used thus when the engine was not running – though one might imag-

ine that the experience of coasting a 56-tonne (55-ton) tank downhill, steering it by differential braking, would have been illuminating to say the least.

The complexity of both the gearbox and the steering unit required scrupulous attention to maintenance procedures if they were to continue to function properly. Not surprisingly, in battlefield conditions this was sometimes difficult to

The tracks, cast from manganese steel, were composed of 96 links, each of which weighed 30kg (66lb) and was joined to its neighbour with a 28mm- (1.1in-) diameter retaining pin. They ran over the drive sprocket, eight sets of 800mm- (31.5in-) diameter wheels and a rear idler (for adjusting track tension) per side; no track return rollers were fitted. Wheels with rubber tyres were fitted to the first production Tigers, but after vehicle No 825 they were replaced by steel-tyred wheels which lasted considerably longer. Each wheel set was composed of three disks, the 'tyres' of which were 75mm (2.96in) wide, arranged as a pair and a singleton, with a space somewhat wider than the combined width of the pair between them. The first wheel set had an inboard pair and an outboard singleton, the second had the arrangement reversed; the second's pair ran in the space in the first (and third) sets, and the arrangement was repeated down the length of the vehicle. This interleaving, which permitted more suspension units to be incorporated, made for a smooth ride, but produced an unforeseen problem: in the severe winters of northern Europe, mud and slush which built up between the interleaved pairs of wheels froze solid after a period of immobility and immobilised the tank. Many Tigers were caught and destroyed in Russia because of this.

CRAMPED AND UNCOMFORTABLE

The build-up of debris, particularly rocks and stones, between the wheel sets also caused Tigers' tracks to ride up over the sprocket teeth and jam solid – the same thing also happened when reversing or turning in boggy conditions. This was a considerable problem, for the resulting tension on the affected track was so great that it could not be freed even by releasing the tension adjustment on the idler wheel, nor could a track pin be driven out. In theory, at least, it was possible to tow a tank thus disabled, but only by putting a massive strain on the towing vehicles – it took three three-quarter tracked 18-tonne (17.7-ton) prime movers (*Zugkraftwagen*) or two Tigers in tandem to pull such a load. Otherwise, the only recourse was to place an explosive charge under the track and blow a link out, though the official position on this somewhat extreme measure was that it should not be attempted unless the alternative was to abandon the vehicle.

Standard Tiger tracks (*Marschketten*) were 725mm (28.6in) wide, which made for a total vehicle width of 3.73m (14.7ft) – too great for the loading gauge of the western European railway system. To allow the tanks to be transported by train, loading tracks (*Verladeketten*), 520mm (20.5in) wide were also available, but in order to fit them the singleton outer wheel of the first, third, fifth and seventh sets had to be removed from each side of the vehicle. The front mudguards, placed at the same angle as the glacis plate and level with it, were made in two parts, and the outer section, which was hinged, could be folded out of the way when the loading tracks were fitted. Entraining and detraining was a lengthy and laborious operation (see box, page 49).

Wide tracks were necessary in order to reduce the ground pressure the Tiger exerted to within manageable limits: 1.04kg/sq cm (14.8lb/sq in) with the combat tracks fitted, but 40 per cent greater on the loading tracks. In comparison,

achieve, and a British Army report of the interrogation of captured Tiger crewmen suggests that failure of the gearbox and steering units was the commonest cause of Tigers breaking down. On one occasion, recounted in some detail later, a 16-strong reinforced company of Tigers, attempting to stem the advance north through Italy, lost no less than 15 of its vehicles in a day – nine of them were destroyed after mechanical failure of the transmissions immobilised them, and two more were abandoned due to their tracks riding up over the sprocket teeth. This figure amounted to almost one-sixth of all the heavy tanks in Italy at the time.

PzKpfw VI Tiger (SdKfz 181) Ausf E

1 8.8cm L/56 gun
2 7.92mm MG34 machine gun
3 7.92mm MG34 machine gun
4 7.92mm machine-gun ammunition
5 Smoke generator discharger
6 Escape hatch
7 Commander's seat
8 Commander's traverse handwheel
9 Revolver port
10 Traverse gearbox
11 Commander's shield
12 Gunner's traverse handwheel
13 Gunner's elevating handwheel
14 Gunner's seat
15 Machine-gun firing pedal
16 Binocular telescope
17 Air cleaning system
18 Maybach engine
19 Radio set
20 88mm ammunition bins
21 Hydraulic traverse foot control

22 Hydraulic traverse unit
23 Disc-brake drum
24 Steering unit
25 Steering wheel
26 Gearbox
27 Driver's seat
28 Handbrake
29 Accelerator
30 Foot brake
31 Clutch
32 Shock absorber
33 Torsion bar suspension
34 Overlapping bogie-wheels
35 Commander's cupola
36 Fan drive clutch lever
37 Air-intake valve control
38 Petrol primer
39 Petrol tap
40 Machine-gun ammunition
   storage

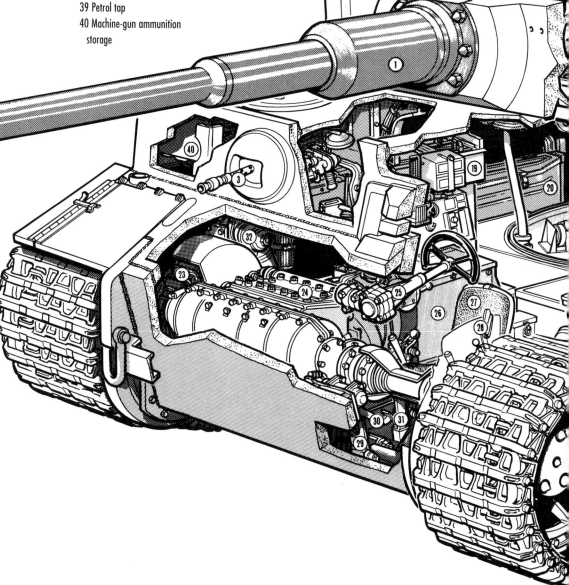

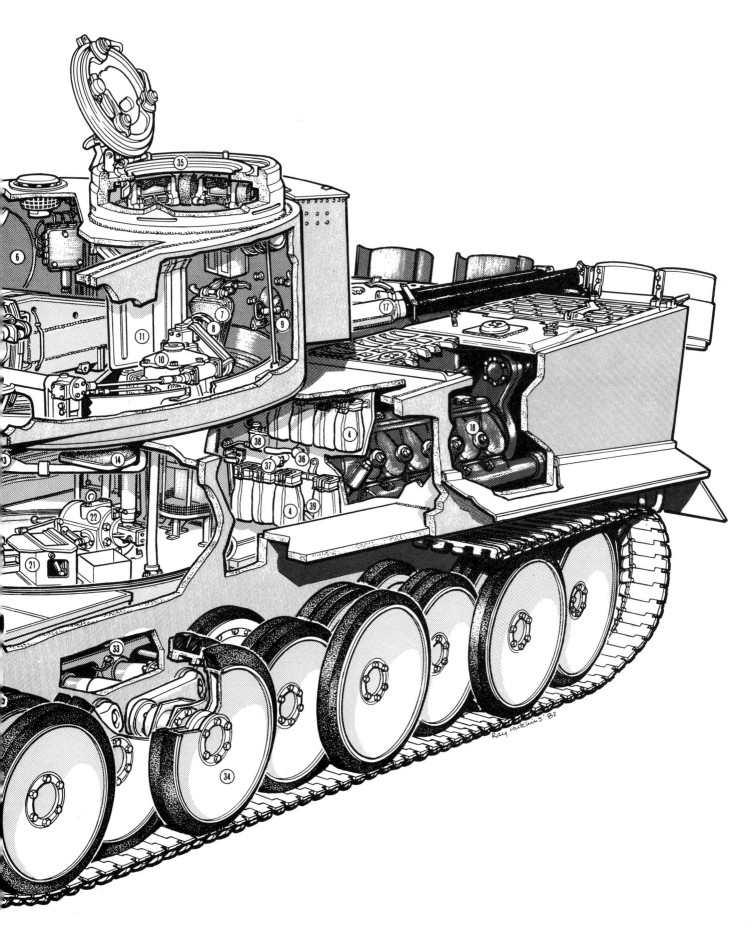

the T-34 exerted a ground pressure of just 0.64kg/sq cm (9lb/sq in), having been designed with operation in the soft terrain of the Ukraine and Byelorussia firmly in mind. This arrangement was superseded from tank number 825 (produced in early March, 1944), and the outer singleton wheels, which had been a constant source of problems, were simply eliminated even when the tank was running on the wide combat tracks.

The tank's suspension was made up of transverse torsion bars, one per wheel set, fixed rigidly to the hull on the side away from the sprung wheel set and located on the suspended side within a fabric bearing, which had to be greased manually at regular intervals. To the torsion bars were fixed trailing-arm stub axles on one side and leading-arm axles on the other, so that the roadwheel sets on opposite sides were square with each other. Each roadwheel ran on paired roller bearings, which were also manually lubricated. Oil-filled shock absorbers were fitted to the front and rearmost wheel sets on each side, which were provided with heavier-gauge torsion bars.

The Tiger tank was divided conventionally into three compartments: the engine at the rear, together with the cooling installation and the fuel tanks; the driver's and bow gunner/radio operator's compartment at the front, where they were separated by the gearbox and steering unit; and the turret, with the main gun and its crew of three – commander, gunner and loader – located centrally. Thanks to the considerable space necessary to accommodate the gun's breech, the turret was reasonably spacious with an internal diameter of 1.8m (5.9ft), though only the loader really benefitted. (This spaciousness was remarked upon in a British Army description of a tank captured in 1943, though that probably says more about current British thinking than about the Tiger.) The breech mechanism itself, including the recoil guide, reached almost to the rear wall of the turret and effectively divided it in two – unequally, since the gun was offset by 100mm (4in) to the right. The 1.45m-

Below: The massive forged breech of the Tiger's 8.8cm KwK36 cannon took up much of the turret space. Suspended on trunnions to the rear of the gun's centre of gravity, it was held in balance by a pair of coil springs. Recoil was minimised by a compensator at the muzzle, the residue absorbed by oil-filled dampers. The best way to disable it was to drain the shock absorbers and fire a single round.

(4.8ft-) diameter turntable slung beneath the turret, which of course turned as it turned, was suspended from three tubular steel pillars attached at the top to the turret ring. On it the hydraulic traversing unit was mounted, there was storage space for petrol cans and a fire extinguisher, and there was an access hatch to the ammunition locker below. The headroom in the turret, measured from the turntable to the turret roof, was 1.55m (5ft). There was an additional 270mm (10.6in) within the cupola on early models; the cupola design was modified in 1944, when the unit designed for the Panther was fitted, with a slight increase in available height.

The gunner's position was forward and to the left, where he was forced to sit with his knees drawn up and leaning over to the right. The loader, opposite him on the far side of the main gun, faced to the rear of the turret. Since he needed to move around more than the other crewmen, in order to delve into the ammunition storage bins, he had considerably more space, and the British Army motion report suggested that his position was the only comfortable one in the entire vehicle.

Behind the gunner, the commander had what was effectively a two-level seat, since the backrest of the lower seat

Above: Since it was considerably heavier than most bridges could bear, the Tiger was designed to ford rivers up to 4.5m (14.7ft) deep, though this required considerable preparation. This tank is ready for total submersion; note the covers over all the apertures in the hull as well as the telescopic 'schnorkel' breathing tube, which supplied air to the crew and the engine.

could be folded out to do duty as a second seat, 1.32m (4.3ft) above the level of the turntable. This was for use when the cupola hatch was open. The higher seat had no backrest, and in this position the commander was somewhat precarious and uncomfortable, having nothing to brace his body against. The lower seat was positioned 0.9m (3ft) above the turntable, so that sitting on it, the commander's head was within the cupola, his eyes level with the ring of five 94mm- (3.7in-) thick laminated glass vision blocks within its body. Two sets of footrests for the commander were positioned on the pillar that held the driver's seat, directly in front of him. He could also stand on the turntable, though to do so he had to contort his body and risked being thrown about if the tank was in motion.

In addition to the vision blocks in the cupola, the commander was provided with a so-called 'scissors' binocular/

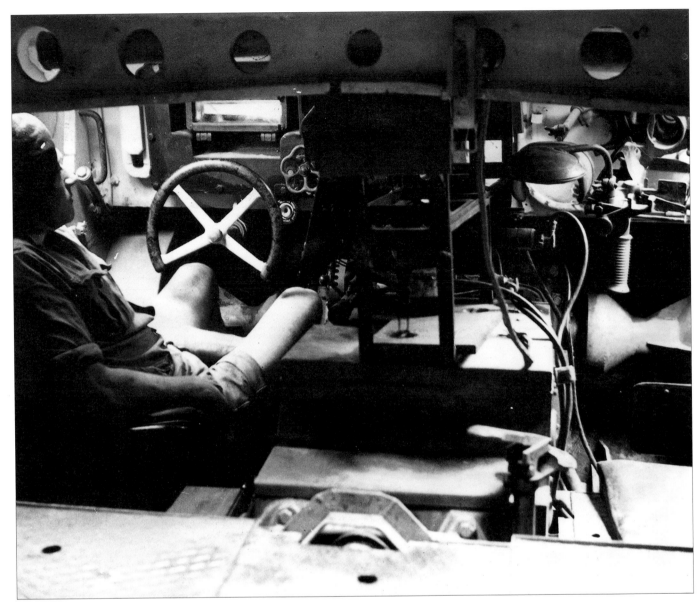

periscope (*Scherenfernrohr*). This was used chiefly to spot the fall of shot rather than to search for targets, since its field of view was restricted. He used it via the hatch, where it could be secured to a support, and could keep his head under cover while doing so. The gunner and loader each had a single vision block in the side wall of the turret, directed 30 degrees left and right respectively. All the vision blocks and episcope/periscopes in the tank were fitted with brow rest/protectors.

DRIVING POSITION

The driver's position, in the front left corner of the hull, was reasonably comfortable save for the inadequate leg room it offered. The other major criticism of it was that the driver had no 'opened-up' position; even in the comparative safety of the rear echelon. His view was through the 94mm- (3.7in-) thick 240 x 70mm (9.5 x 2.8in) visor in the front plate. This was equipped with double sliding shutter doors which moved in the vertical plane, operated by a handwheel mounted to the right of the steering wheel. The field of view was only adequate when the doors were fully open.

Above: Much of the forward crew compartment, which housed the driver on the left and the hull gunner/wireless operator on the right, was taken up by the transmission located between them. Each man had an escape hatch above his head, but there was no provision for either to man his position with his head above it – and visibility, via vision blocks and periscopes, was very limited.

The driver was also provided with a fixed episcope/periscope with a 125 x 35mm (4.9 x 1.4in) aperture, mounted in the access hatch above his head, which pointed 30 degrees to the left, though this seems to have been deleted by mid-1944. His seat was adjustable fore-and-aft and for rake, and the backrest could be let down to allow him access to the turret – so as to be able to pass up the replenishment of ammunition held in the bin to his left. He had a conventional steering wheel and pedals for the accelerator, brakes and clutch, while levers to his right and left controlled the brakes individually, and thus could be used to steer the tank in an emergency.

The bow gunner's position was a mirror-image of the driver's, though his seat was fixed and somewhat smaller. Apart from the limited leg room and the discomfort caused by the head pan of the gun pressing down on him, he would have been reasonably comfortable. In addition to the telescope sight for the machine gun, he was provided with an episcope/periscope which, like the driver's, was located in the hatch above his head and was angled at 30 degrees out from the fore-and-aft line of the vehicle. The Fu5 inter-vehicle radio, the operation of which was his other responsibility, was easily accessible, being mounted atop the gearbox immediately to his left.

ACCESS HATCHES

In addition to the cupola hatch and the two hatches located forward of the turret, which were located above the driver and bow gunner's heads and gave access to their positions, the loader was also provided with a hatch above his position. This not only provided access to his position but allowed him to dispose of used shell cases. (It could also be used as an ammunition loading hatch, and, in fact was the only means of so doing in early production models.) Unlike the other hatches, which were all circular, the loader's hatch was rectangular. Hinged at the front, it was actuated by a sprung piston and arm which were mounted on the underside of the

turret roof and frequently proved a nuisance. Like the loader's hatch, those for the bow gunner and driver were also spring-loaded. They opened sideways and almost flat to the hull. The commander's hatch in the cupola, in contrast, opened only to just over the vertical, to the right-hand side; it gave the commander a measure of lateral protection, but increased the effective height of the vehicle considerably when it was open. In later production models of the Tiger, late in 1943, there was a circular emergency hatch located in the right rear quarter of the turret wall; hinged at the bottom, it dropped down when opened (obstructing the turret's traverse in the process), and could not then be closed again from inside the tank. It was used to load ammunition into the tank as well as to provide an alternative exit route *in extremis*.

The British motion study report noted that it took the bow gunner, the driver and the loader some seven seconds to

Below: The driving position was quite conventional, with wheel, pedals and gearshift (the notched quadrant to the right of the steering wheel) all placed very nearly where you would expect to find them in a car or truck. The seat was adjustable fore-and-aft and for rake, and the back could be let down to allow access to the driving position from the turret.

Above: The hull gunner/wireless operator's position. Somewhat smaller than the driver's position, the hull gunner's post was actually one of the more comfortable in the Tiger, though his legs were forced over to the right by the transmission housing. The cup fixed to the machine gun mount rested on his head, and since the gun was breech-heavy, caused considerable discomfort.

evacuate the tank, using the hatches above their heads, while the commander could exit through the cupola hatch in nine seconds, followed three seconds later by the gunner, who alone had no hatch of his own.

An automatic fire-suppression system was fitted to the engine compartment. Detection was by means of bimetal thermostats set to trigger at 120 degrees C (248 degrees F), located at the carburettor air intakes and adjacent to the fuel pumps, which acted through a solenoid to open the delivery valve on a pressurised vessel containing three litres (.79 US gallons/.64 UK gallons)of carbon tetrachloride, which was piped to four spray nozzles. A clockwork timer shut down the suppression system after seven seconds, but it would be immediately retriggered if the area had not cooled sufficiently by then. The system had sufficient capacity to allow five suppression cycles.

We have seen how the Tiger's designers solved the problem of reducing the ground pressure the tank exerted while at the same time permitting it to be transported by rail, by laboriously swopping combat tracks for loading tracks (see below for an account of the procedure involved). The way they got around the problem of the weight limit of bridges was rather more radical. They designed the tank to be able to operate entirely submerged, in up to 4.5m (14.76ft) of water, so that it could cross most European rivers under its own power. All the tank's hatches, including the engine access hatches, were fitted with rubber seals, while the turret ring was sealed by an inflatable rubber tube. The mushroom ventilator situated in the upper hull plate between the driver's and bow gunner's hatches, which functioned as an air intake for the crew space, could be sealed shut, while the stale-air outlet was fitted with a non-return flap valve.

The radiator compartments at the very rear were isolated from the engine proper, the air intake to which (also a mushroom ventilator) could be sealed shut, and they were flooded as the tank submerged (the drive to the fans which sucked air through the radiators having been disconnected). Lastly, a four-piece telescopic standpipe or *schnörkel* was erected on the engine compartment cover to satisfy the needs of both crew and powerplant; exhaust gases were discharged directly into the water, via nonreturn valves incorporated into the silencers. A mechanical bilge pump, driven off the auxiliary gearbox that provided power to the turret traverse system, was fitted to remove any water that seeped in.

SUBMERSIBLE ATTRIBUTES

Though the Tiger tank was clearly designed, rather than simply adapted, to be submersible, doubts have been expressed whether the design was entirely successful. Late in 1944 or at the very start of 1945, British troops captured a German order expressly forbidding the submersion of tanks, and newer tanks captured some time before had not been equipped with some of the necessary items. This is not necessarily conclusive proof of the system's failure, however, since by that time the German Army was on the defensive, and was slowly being driven back everywhere (the brief success in the Ardennes, notwithstanding) over territory it already knew. This effectively removed the need to cross rivers on untried bridges of unknown capacity, and rendered the deep-wading equipment surplus to requirements. It may well have been that the system worked after a fashion, but was not completely reliable, and was therefore deleted when not necessary.

The combination of the regenerative steering unit and the OLVAR gearbox made driving the Tiger relatively straightforward, despite its great size and weight. Driving a PzKpfw III or IV, which weighed less than half as much, but had differential steering and manual gearboxes, was considerably more difficult and physically very tiring. If the Tiger's steering system had an operational drawback, it lay in the inherent nature of the regenerative system – when the engine was running, even with the gearshift in neutral, turning the steering wheel would cause the entire vehicle to turn about its axis. Thus, the driver had to take very considerable pains not to touch the steering wheel accidentally when the engine was running, particularly when getting in and out of his seat.

Selecting the direction of travel and changing gear were two quite separate and independent operations, each one controlled by its own lever, both of them mounted, naturally enough, on the gearbox itself, adjacent to the driver's right hand. Both were simple fore-and-aft arcs, with notches for each position. The direction selection lever had three positions – *Vorwärts* (Forward), *Leerlauf* (Neutral) and *Rückwärts* (Reverse). Forward allowed any of the eight gears to be selected, while Reverse only allowed the driver to select from the lower half of the range, between first and fourth gears. The gear selector had eight positions. Neutral could not be selected when the tank was moving forward in the top half of the range. This was a deliberate safety device, since in Neutral the tank would spin around on its tracks if the driver turned the steering wheel. When one of the ratios in the lower range was selected, in either direction, the procedure to brake or downshift was to put the selector into Neutral first. From a higher gear, the driver declutched instead before applying the brakes and bringing the vehicle to a stop.

SWITCHING GEARS

To start off from rest, the driver declutched and selected Forward or Reverse, then selected a gear between first and fourth, depending on the terrain – on a hillside, in soft ground, for example, he would select first gear; on a level, hard-surfaced road, fourth. He depressed the accelerator until the engine was turning over in excess of 1600rpm, and then let in the clutch, and the vehicle moved off. From then on, it was unnecessary to use the clutch to change up and down through the gears; the driver simply lifted off the accelerator, changed to the desired gear and depressed the accelerator again. It was not necessary to go from gear to gear sequentially; one could change from fourth to sixth, for example. All that was necessary was for the gear selected to keep engine speed above 1600rpm, the point at which the flow of oil from the gearbox pumps dropped below the level necessary to operate the clutches, and below the maximum speed to which the engine was governed.

Matching engine speed to road speed, and knowing which gear he should change to in order to keep the engine revolutions at the optimum level as conditions changed, was probably the most difficult part of the driver's task. (The recommended point at which to change down was 1700rpm, and it was normal to change up at 2300rpm, and 600rpm is a very narrow power band even in such a ponderous powerplant.) It was generally necessary to use engine braking when going downhill; accelerating downhill was strictly forbidden, not least because the engine governor did not operate when the tank was in a nose-down attitude, and even fairly minimal overrevving was a sure way to inflict serious damage on an engine with such heavy reciprocating components.

Aware of the narrowness of the safety margins in an engine which would regularly be called on to operate at its limits, Maybach did his best to reduce the possibility of poor driving technique or nonadherence to the rigourous maintenance schedule damaging the powerplant by incorporating dry sump lubrication and using roller bearings wherever possible. However, the best design in the world can never compensate for ill-use, and it is certain that Tigers spent more time than was desirable in the workshop, though most of the mechanical failures recorded were to be found within the very complex transmission system, rather than in the engine.

CHAPTER 3

Tiger Tank Unit Organisation and Combat Tactics

The development of the Tiger heavy tank caused a considerable upheaval in the organisation of Germany's armoured divisions. Initially, it was planned to use the new tanks in mixed platoons, alongside PzKpfw III and IV medium tanks, but that plan was soon shelved.

Soon after the decision to produce a heavy tank was taken, and even before their operating characteristics became known, changes were made to the table of organisation of the German Army and Waffen-SS Panzer Divisions to accommodate them. The first step was to establish heavy-tank companies (*schwere Panzerkompanien* – s.Pz.Kp) as independent units (*Heerestruppen*), composed of three platoons [*Zuge*] with three PzKpfw VIs each. Initially there were two heavy tank companies, 501st and 502nd, created on 16 February 1942. The two were united and remustered as 1 and 2 Companies/501st Heavy Panzer Battalion (*schwere Panzerabteilung*) on 10 May. Confusingly, 503rd Heavy Panzer Battalion had actually been formed five days earlier, and was thus, nominally at least, the German Army's senior heavy tank battalion – 502nd Heavy Panzer Battalion was created two weeks later.

It was initially intended that the 501st and 503rd Heavy Panzer Battalions should be equipped with PzKpfw VI(P)s, and sent to North Africa, and that the 502nd should be equipped with PzKpfw VI(H)s, and sent to the Eastern Front. The Porsche-produced PzKpfw VI(P) was cancelled, resulting in a delay while the 501st and 503rd Heavy Panzer Battalions were retrained on the very different Henschel tank. Thus it was that the 502nd Heavy Panzer Battalion became the first Tiger-equipped unit to go into action.

The pioneering units had vehicles before they began to receive Tigers, of course. In April 1942, a decision had been taken that each Tiger tank sent into action should be accompanied by a PzKpfw III to provide security, and Wartime Organisation Table (*Kriegsstärkenachweisung*) 1176 was drawn up accordingly and issued 25 April. A total of 10 PzKpfw III (75)s were issued, to make up four-platoon companies

Left: Said to be the first photograph of a Tiger tank ever published (in April 1943, but it was probably taken quite some time earlier), this is one of the 10 heavy tanks that *8.Kp/SS-Pz.Rgt. 2* took to Russia in February 1943, for the successful counteroffensive around Kharkov. This type lacks cyclone air filters.

when their heavy tanks were finally delivered. The PzKpfw III (75) was a PzKpfw III Ausf N with the short L/24 7.5cm gun, capable of firing high explosive, high explosive anti-tank, smoke and anti-personnel rounds. It was often known as PzKpfw III Kz (Kz for *kurz*, meaning short).

The 502nd Heavy Panzer Battalion was to have four PzKpfw VIs in each of two platoons and five PzKpfw III Kzs in each of the other two, with one PzKpfw VI in the Company Headquarters, while the combat companies of the 501st and 503rd Heavy Panzer Battalions had two PzKpfw VIs and two PzKpfw III Kzs in each platoon, and one PzKpfw VI along with two PzKpfw III Kzs in the Company Headquarters (*Kompanie-Truppe*). This arrangement was formalised in the Wartime Organisation Table 1176d of 15 August 1942.

MIXED PANZER COMPANIES

Alongside this, the battalion's Headquarters Company (*Stabskompanie*) was organised according to Wartime Organisation Table 1150d of the same date, with two Tiger command tanks (*Panzerbefehlswagen*) and a PzKpfw III Ausf L, with the KwK39 5cm L/60 gun, known as the PzKpfw III Lg (Lg for *lang*, meaning long) in its Signals Platoon (*Nachrichtenzug*), and five PzKpfw III Lgs in a separate platoon. Four months later, the first Tigers had gone into battle, and an amended table of organisation was issued, swopping the PzKpfw III Kzs in the combat companies for PzKpfw III Lgs.

The original battalions had two combat companies each, but were upgraded to three during the first trimester of 1943. The 502nd Heavy Panzer Battalion lost its 2 Company, which became 3 Company/503rd Heavy Panzer Battalion on 10 February, and got new 2 and 3 Companies on 1 April. Possibly because it was treated as an experimental unit, 1 Company/502nd Heavy Panzer Battalion had an anomalous table of organisation. It received nine PzKpfw III Lgs to supplement its nine III Kzs in late September 1942, and records show that it continued to operate all three types of tank until the latter part of 1943. The 505th Heavy Panzer Battalion also operated both types of PzKpfw III alongside its Tigers on the Eastern Front until Operation *Zitadelle* (the offensive at Kursk) in July 1943.

In general, however, the PzKpfw III Lgs proved to be no more effective than the Ausf Ns, and the Wartime Organisation Table 1176e of 5 March 1943 ordered that the strength of each company was to be increased to 14 PzKpfw VIs, organised in three platoons of four tanks each, together with a *Kompanie-Truppe* of two tanks. Also, each battalion had a signals platoon equipped with one standard PzKpfw VI and two others transformed into command tanks (SdKfz 267/268 *Panzerbefehlswagen*) with additional radio equipment in place of some of their ammunition storage bins. In all, total battalion strength numbered 45 tanks.

Below: This picture, taken somewhere in northern Germany in 1945, of a Tiger alongside one of its main adversaries, a British Cromwell (probably a Mk IV), shows clearly the huge difference in size between the two. An attempt may have been made to recover the Tiger, for a towing cable is attached to one of the front eyes.

Above: By the style in which its tactical number is painted (variations on which are often the only means of placing a tank in a particular unit), this Tiger seems to have been part of *s.Pz.Abt. 503*, 2nd Company. It is halted on a road march and is equipped with some very nonstandard items atop its turret.

Despite the protests of most of the unit commanders involved, the PzKpfw IIIs were withdrawn from all except 1 Company/502nd and 505th Heavy Panzer Battalions and were replaced with half-tracked armoured infantry carriers (*Leichter Schützenpanzerwagen*, SdKfz 250), assigned to the battalion headquarters company for scouting and perimeter guard duties. These changes were largely completed on the Eastern Front by the start of Operation *Zitadelle*.

The reasons for this reorganisation were both tactical and logistical. The PzKpfw IIIs had been assigned to act as the Tigers' 'minders', and were simply not up to the task – a fact which should have been obvious all along, since the inadequacies of the medium tanks had been the reason for rushing the Tiger into production in the first place. In addition, the presence of two types of tank within each company put a considerable burden on the companies' Vehicle Maintenance Section (*Kraftfahrzeug-Instandsetzungsgruppe*) and the battalion's Workshop Company (*Werkstatt-Kompanie*), and eliminating the medium tank simplified the task considerably. However, this did not mean the end of PzKpfw IIIs and IVs, only that the medium tanks were not now expected to defend the Tigers.

In all, 11 heavy tank battalions were to be created within the German Army, numbering 501 to 510, together with the 3rd Battalion/*Grossdeutschland* Panzer Regiment. The latter was made up of the remnants of the 501st Battalion and 504th Battalion, together with one re-equipped company of the regiment itself. Units were formed as and when vehicles to equip them came off the production lines, and the last

battalion to be formed, 510th, was not created until 6 June 1944, the day the Allies landed in Normandy. During the course of the war, some units' designations were changed: the reconstituted 501st became Heavy Panzer Battalion 424 in November 1944; the 502nd was redesignated 511th on 5 January 1945 and the 503rd was renamed Heavy Panzer Battalion *Feldherrnhalle* on 21 December 1944.

Late in the war, the tanks allocated to Reserve Army training units were pressed into combat service; these units were equipped, as one might imagine, with a mix of the vehicles to be found on active service, including some Tigers. A total of 30 Tigers (some reports suggest more) and 15 King Tigers were shipped to army training units in total, including the 14 Tigers which went to Paderborn before September 1944 (see below), and a further eight which went to SS training units. Tiger tanks were allocated to radio-control (*Funklenk*) units, which were trained to deploy unmanned, remotely controlled half-tracked vehicles – SdKfz 301 *Sprengstoffträger* – packed with explosives. The radio-controlled units were never successful, and what remained of them was thrown into the fighting in 1945 in the conventional role. When the Panzer-Lehr Division was formed in January 1944, from a collection of smaller Panzer-Lehr units, some of the 10 Tiger tanks that

Above: Apparently still serviceable after taking a great number of hits from Soviet anti-tank guns (the original German caption to this picture states that it is just about to go into action) this Tiger demonstrates quite effectively just why the tank's crews felt so invulnerable.

Right: Pictured near Ternopol in the Ukraine, probably in March or April, 1944, these older Tigers (note the early twin apertures for the binocular gun-sight), perhaps from *s.Pz.Abt. 506*, show signs of hard use but little battle damage. Note, too, the main gun ammunition boxes on the turret top.

had been issued to the 130th Panzer-Lehr Regiment the previous October formed part of the division's table of organisation, though they never amounted to a full company.

The Waffen-SS was authorised to create heavy tank companies on 13 November 1942, one for each of the SS-Panzer Regiments 1st, 2nd and 3rd, which formed part of the *Leibstandarte SS Adolf Hitler, Das Reich* and *Totenkopf* Divisions respectively. They were to be organised in the same way as the army companies, with nine Tigers each. All three companies were up to strength by the end of January 1943. When the revised table of organisation, 1176e, was issued the following March, they were each issued with five more tanks. The SS heavy tank companies were expanded into battalions during the summer of 1943, and became the 101st to 103rd SS Heavy Panzer Battalions. They were later (in September 1944) redesignated 501st to 503rd SS Heavy Panzer Battalions, which caused some confusion since there were army heavy tank battalions of the same numerical designation; the latter were redesignated as a result, as described above. After this reorganisation, the 1st, 2nd and 3rd SS Panzer Regiments retained heavy tank companies of their own.

INDEPENDENT COMMANDS

What we would today call combat teams, equipped with a variety of armoured vehicles including Tigers, were also set up, and were usually known by the name of their leader. *Tigergruppe Meyer* and *Panzerkompanie Hummel* were the best known – but they were short-lived, being absorbed later into existing units.

Hummel Heavy Panzer Company (first known as *Einsatz Dunkirchen* Heavy Panzer Company; its name was changed after three days) was hastily formed on 17 September 1944 out of the 500th Heavy Panzer Reserve and Training Battalion at Paderborn, and equipped with the 14 Tiger tanks available there. It was sent west to Arnhem on 19 September to reinforce elements of the Waffen-SS *Hohenstauffen* and *Frundsberg* Divisions (9th and 10th SS Panzer Divisions) and 506th Heavy Panzer Battalion, which had just been re-established and issued with new King Tigers. It had gone to the area to train and found itself in action when it was thrown into the battle to counter the Allied Operation 'Market Garden' – the attempt to sieze a crossing over the Lower Rhine by means of airborne landings and a narrow-front penetration. On 8 December, instead of being returned to training duties, *Panzerkompanie Hummel* was incorporated into the 506th Heavy Panzer Battalion as its 4 Company, and the 500th Reserve Battalion received new (probably rebuilt) vehicles.

TIGER UNIT STRENGTHS

If all the heavy tank battalions had been up to strength all the time, then the number of Tigers in the field at any one time would have reached over 700. From March 1944, that included King Tigers, though the first five of these tanks to be issued, to 316 Radio-Control Company, attached to the Panzer-Lehr Division and stationed in Normandy, were so unreliable that the Panzer-Lehr Division reported to the Inspector-General of Armoured Forces, Heinz Guderian, that: 'In the event of combat employment, the danger exists that they will fall into enemy hands due to mechanical breakdown. Therefore, for security reasons, the division requests that these five Tiger IIs be sent to a unit in Germany where further troop trials can be conducted.' There is no record of the fate of these five tanks. In fact, in only one month – July 1944 – did the total inventory reach 700, largely thanks to production in April and May topping 100 tanks per month. On 1 July there were 671 operational Tigers and 55 operational King Tigers.

July 1944 was also the blackest month for the heavy tank battalions: they lost 195 Tigers. As a result the inventory for 1 August stood at 549, the difference having been made up with new and rebuilt tanks. From then on numbers steadily dwindled. In total, 1350 Tiger tanks were produced between 1942 and 1944, of which six were tested to destruction. Records show that 1413 Tigers were issued to combat and training units, and the apparent discrepancy is accounted for by the tanks returned to the factory at Kassel for rebuilding (69), which were subsequently reissued as new. Most surviving

PROBLEMS OF STRATEGIC MOBILITY

Before the days of two- and three-lane dual carriageways, when specially constructed articulated trucks could be used to transport tanks at relatively high speed over long distances, the only means to do so were the railways. This meant that tank designers were routinely constrained by what is known as the loading gauge.

From very early on in the development process, it was clear that in order to maintain a reasonable ground pressure level, the Tiger tank would need tracks that would be too wide to allow it to remain within the loading gauge of the Western European railway system. The problem was overcome by designing a separate narrow set of tracks, to be employed when the tank was being transported by train. The effect of this unavoidable design decision was to be a back-breaking job for the men tasked with actually loading and unloading these monsters at railheads.

Under ideal conditions, where a train could be reversed up to an end-ramp, the actual loading and unloading itself could be accomplished quite easily, but even so, the entire process was a slow one, because the tanks' tracks had to be changed twice, once at each end. To accomplish a change from standard tracks (*Marschketten*) to loading tracks (*Verladeketten*), the latter, which were part of the equipment of the flatcar, not of the tank, were first towed off the car by a tractor (*Zugkraftwagen*) and laid out on the ground in front of the tank, parallel and the correct distance apart, but in echelon, not side-by-side. One standard track was then disconnected, and the tank was driven forward on one track only, so that the bogie wheels on the non-driven side ran off the broad track and onto the narrow. The tank moved forward until the far end of the narrow track was between the sprocket and the first roadwheel, with the narrow track extending out behind the vehicle. In order to effect the link up, a wire cable was attached to the far end, led forwards above the roadwheels and a turn taken around the sprocket wheel, which now functioned as a capstan. With the drive switched to this side only, the crew tailed on the cable, and slowly the narrow track was drawn forwards to the sprocket, where the link could be made. The procedure was then repeated for the other track.

All that remained now was to recover the standard tracks. First, the tractor towed them to a point where they lay side by side, between the Tiger and the loading ramp. The Tiger then drove forwards, so as to straddle the tracks on the ground, and wire ropes were attached to the lifting eyes at the front of the turret, led forward over the frontal armour and secured to the forward end of the tracks. The Tiger drove up the ramp and onto the flatcar, towing its tracks beneath itself; a second pair of cables was then attached to the free end of the tracks, to be led, via a pair of pulleys in front of the tank, to the tractor winch, which dragged the rear of the tracks up over the rear deck of the tank, where they were secured.

A pair of standard tracks weighed 5.75 tonnes (5.64 tons), and a pair of travelling tracks four tonnes (3.94 tons). A small number of 80-tonne (78.7-ton) capacity road trailers were constructed to transport Tigers; they were employed in an almost identical manner to the railway flatcars.

Above: A later-model Tiger Ausf E, probably dated mid-1944 as the grenade throwers and smoke dischargers are missing, it has a single central driving light, monocular gunsight and newer wheels. Note the design of the commander's cupola. The tank is covered in *zimerit* paste to protect against magnetic grenades.

Below: An *SS-Hauptscharführer* (senior sergeant-major) with the 2nd SS-Panzer Division *Das Reich*. Presumably he is the commander of this early model Tiger. Note the distinctive divisional sign on the Tiger tank in the background.

examples were cut up for scrap after the end of the war, and by the 1950s, just four were known to exist.

TIGER TACTICS

The first heavy tank companies were committed to battle on an ad hoc basis, as vehicles became available, thereby achieving little but giving away the precious element of surprise that an impenetrable shroud of secrecy had given them. The result was something of a fiasco. Certainly, at that time, very little thought or guidance had been given to developing tactics.

As a result, the men of the first units – 501st, 502nd and 503rd Heavy Panzer Battalions – were left largely to their own devices, with only the experience gained earlier in light- and medium-tank units to guide them. Not unnaturally, the development of tactics was a priority, and regular reports were demanded of the unit commanders. The results were Training Pamphlets (*Merkblatten*) 47a/29 and /30, issued on 20 May 1943, after the reorganisation into the definitive 14-tank company structure. The pamphlets were to be used in conjunction with the appropriate manuals for the training and employment of existing medium-tank units. They are worth quoting at some length since they rep-

resent both the German Army's experience of operating the Tiger, and its aspirations for the vehicle. Some of the assertions made in the documents must have appeared more than a little unrealistic to the experienced tankers who were to crew the new vehicles. The two pamphlets appear to be the work of different hands, and the pamphlet aimed at more senior battalion commanders is, perhaps not surprisingly, considerably more mature.

TRAINING PAMPHLET 47A/29 FOR TRAINING AND EMPLOYMENT OF THE TIGER HEAVY PANZER COMPANY

A. Purpose, tasks and organisation of the Heavy Panzer Company

1 Great firepower, strong armour, high terrain-crossing ability, even in winter, and strong overrunning power are the characteristics of the heavy tanks ... They enable the company to:

• attack in the first wave against strong defences
• destroy heavy enemy tanks and other armoured targets at long range
• defeat enemy defences decisively
• break through reinforced defensive positions.

2. The heavy tank companies are the strongest combat weapons in the armoured forces (*Panzerwaffe*). As a rule they will be employed within the heavy tank battalion to overcome enemy resistance and break into his defensive positions by utilising concentrated effective fire superiority, protected by strong armour.

3. The great weight of the heavy tank makes it unable to use many bridges, calls for the reinforcing of others and the availability of special bridging and road-making equipment and the advance scouting of possible fording places...

C. The individual PzKpfw VI

6. The PzKpfw VI accomplishes its combat mission within the platoon in two-tank sections or as individual vehicles to guard the rest and assembly areas of its own units. The loss of the platoon leader or section leader, rapidly changing conditions, as well as close terrain can often demand that vehicles be handled individually.

7. With its main weapon, the PzKpfw VI engages as priority:

• Armoured targets and bunker embrasures [with armour-piercing ammunition]
• Nests of resistance, anti-tank guns, artillery positions and massed targets [with HE ammunition].

The long range of the 8.8cm gun makes it possible to engage targets effectively at long distances.

8. Using a gunner's quadrant, long-range fire is possible at distances of up to 9000m [5.6 miles], but long-range deployment against artillery or massed targets is only practical at ranges up to 5000m [3.1 miles] and then only if the tank cannot close the targets because of barriers or terrain obstacles.

9. The 8.8cm gun will be fired while [the tank is] halted. The [vehicle] is to be brought into [the] firing position with its front approximately facing towards the enemy fire [striking angle and thicker protection]. Take up hidden and hull-down firing positions.

10. The flat trajectory of the 8.8cm rounds requires special attention to safety when firing over our own troops.

11. With the turret and hull machine guns, the PzKpfw VI engages unarmoured targets at close and short ranges [up to 400m (440yds) for the former, half that

Below: An unusual picture of an entire company of Tigers drawn up in line-ahead formation. Since all the tanks shown are early models, the picture was probably taken during 1943. Note the cables already attached to the forward towing eyes – to minimise the time necessary to tow away a damaged vehicle.

for the latter]. Massed targets can also be successfully engaged at ranges of up to 800m [880yds].

D. The Platoon

I. General

12. The Platoon Leader [*Zugführer*, usually a senior sergeant – an *Oberfeldwebel* in the Army, an *SS-Scharführer* or *SS-Hauptscharführer* in the Waffen-SS] is responsible for the combat readiness of his platoon. Following orders from the Company Commander, he leads the platoon by radio, signals and example.

13. The platoon consists of four tanks. It is organised as two sections. During separate employment the Platoon Leader commands the first section, the Section Leader the second…

III. Combat

15. The platoon is a unit within the company. Employment with or attachment to a Medium-Tank Company [equipped with PzKpfw III or IVs] or Panzer Grenadiers [an infantry unit deployed with armoured vehicles] creates an exception. It may be necessary to reinforce medium tanks for special missions [as the point element], or to support infantry by crossing rivers and engaging a reinforced defensive position.

16. The platoon conducts an attack by continually shifting rapidly between fire and movement. The section and individual tanks mutually support and guard each other's advance. Short halts to fire and rapid movement to the next firing position are recommended. Long bounds are to be made; never under 200m

Above: Men of the Pioneer Company of *s.Pz.Abt. 505* attempt to improve a crossing point in swampy terrain during the run-up to Operation *Zitadelle*. Terrain like this consistently defeated Tigers, which soon dug themselves in if they tried to cross.

[220yds]. The direction of travel and the firing positions are to be changed frequently by utilising cover offered by the terrain.

E. The Company

IV. Marches

20. The march route requires especially thorough scouting because of the width, length [especially of the gun] and weight of the heavy tank. Aerial photographs are to be used to spot hairpin curves, narrow-angled streets in villages and narrows.

In general, the PzKpfw VI can drive over every short bridge that will carry the PzKpfw IV.

21. On long stretches, the Tiger company cannot march within the columns of motorised or other panzer units, especially not in unknown terrain, because bridges and narrows can be obstacles for the Tigers, which will endanger the flow of the march for the entire unit.

22. During night marches, especially on dark nights, it is useful to have a crew member sit on the forward outer corner of the track guards of the heavy tank in order to instruct the driver by shouting through the open driver's hatch.

23. The heavy tank requires many maintenance halts. A maintenance halt is to be ordered after the first 5km [three miles], and then every 10–15km [6–9 miles].

24. Basically, soft lanes should be used for marches, because hard surfaces and high road crowns cause heavy stress on the running gear, particularly on the inner roadwheels.

The average speed for a daytime march is to be 10–15kmph [6–9mph], by night 7–10kmph [4.4–6mph].

V. Preparing for action

25. The unmistakable howling of the heavy tank's engine [which can be heard at especially] long distances at night, requires consideration of wind direction and that assembly areas be located some distance from the front in order to preserve the element of surprise.

26. After leaving the assembly area it is often necessary to take a short halt within our own lines to refuel…

27. After driving into the assembly area the identifying wide and deep tracks and furrows made by the heavy tank must be eradicated to conceal the presence of the vehicles from enemy aerial reconnaissance.

28. If the assembly area must be entered during the day, the company is to be widely dispersed. During marches heavy tanks are to be camouflaged with branches or tarpaulins.

VI. Combat

A. Attacks

29. The strength of the heavy tank company's attack lies in concentrated employment within the battalion.

30. As a rule, the company's attack formation is the broad wedge [*Breitkeil*, see below].

31. Continually switching between fire and movement, the company breaks into the enemy's position; charges through the enemy zone of resistance; engages and silences armoured targets, defensive weapons, nests of resistance and heavy weapons, and destroys the enemy artillery. It is important to destroy every anti-tank weapon within the company's combat sector.

32. The Company Commander [usually an *Oberleutnant* in the Army, or an *SS-Obersturmführer* in the Waffen-SS] must strive to bring all of the weapons of the heavy tank company to unified effect.

33. Flank protection requires special attention.

VII. Tank versus tank combat

34. The most important task of the heavy tank company is to engage enemy tanks. This always has priority over every other assignment.

35. Independent, swift handling by the Company Commander and strict control of the company with short clear orders are the basis for success. Immediate attack is usually the best solution.

36. The enemy is to be repeatedly deceived and confused by constant changes in the methods of attack. The following tactics aid in this:

a. Opening fire from ambush out of favourable positions [hull-down, or positions along the edges of forest, towns, etc.] at maximum effective range and from unexpected directions.

b. During counterattacks by enemy tanks, build a fire

Below: An impromptu staff conference aboard a Tiger of *1.Kp.s.Pz.Abt 504*, Italy, summer 1944. The distinctive corrugated pattern is the sawdust-based *Zimmerit* paste, applied to prevent mines from sticking to the tank's armour.

PzKpfw VI Tiger Ausf H/E

FACTS AND FIGURES

Crew	five
Weight	50.5 tonnes (49.7 tons)
Hull length	6.3m (20.66ft)
Length, gun forward	8.45m (27.72ft)
Width	3.72m (12.2ft)
Height	3m (9.8ft)
Average road speed	40kmph (25mph)
Maximum range	195km (120 miles)
Powerplant	one Maybach petrol engine
Main armament	one 8.8cm Kwk36 rifled cannon
Secondary armament	two 7.92mm MG34 machine guns, one coaxially mounted, one hull mounted
Ancillary armament	one 7.92mm MG34 anti-aircraft machine gun, one 9mm MP38 or MP40 machine pistol, 9mm P38 pistols
Armour	rolled homogenous nickel steel plate

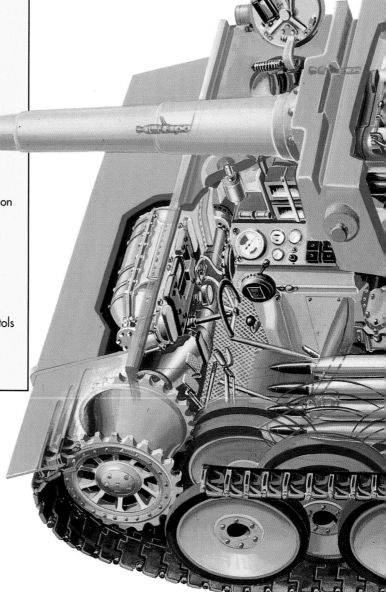

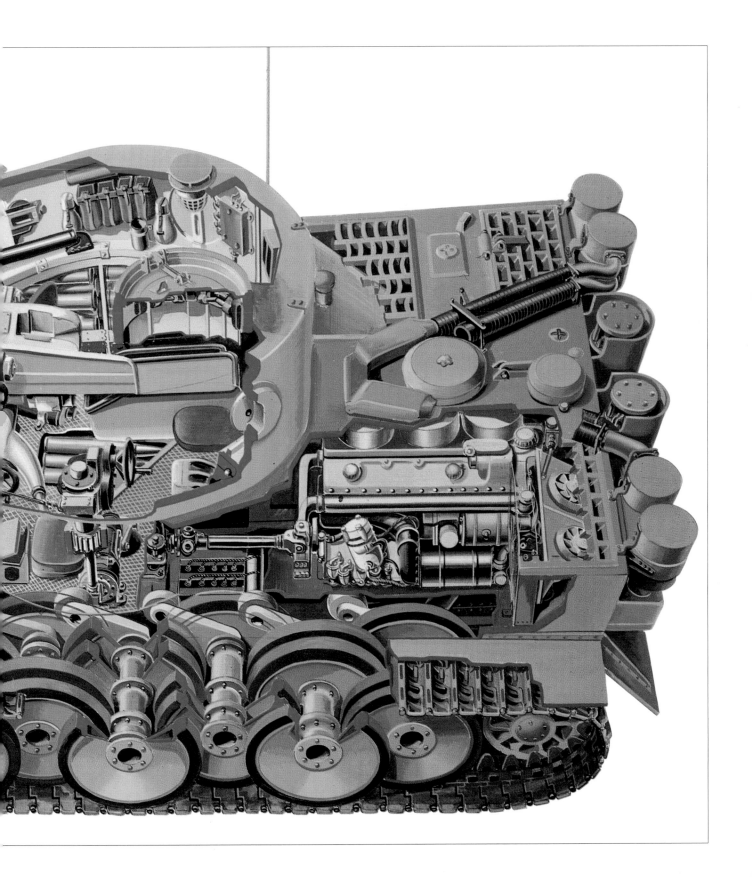

front and send elements to engage them with flanking fire. Let the enemy tanks close the range. Shut down the engines in order to hear better. Destroy the enemy with a counterstrike.

c. Surround or bypass through difficult terrain.

d. Go into action against the flanks and rear by exploiting the sun's position, wind direction and ground cover.

e. If a strong defensive front is unexpectedly encountered, along with [anti-]tank obstacles, immediately withdraw from enemy fire and renew the attack from an unexpected position. Use smoke skilfully.

f. During attacks in close terrain or fights in built-up areas, send out infantry or reconnaissance troops on foot to locate enemy tanks early and determine a favourable attack direction, or gain a favourable firing position while advancing under mutually supporting covering fire.

g. Withdrawing enemy tanks are to be pursued without delay and destroyed.

37. Knocked-out or immobilised enemy tanks are to be blown up during retreats.

TRAINING PAMPHLET 47A/30 FOR THE EMPLOYMENT OF THE TIGER HEAVY PANZER BATTALIONS

A. Purpose, tasks and organisation of the Heavy Panzer Battalion

Its weapons and armour, in combination with its high manoeuvrability, make the Tiger the most powerful combat weapon in the armoured forces.

The Tiger battalion is therefore a powerful decisive-

point weapon … Its strength lies in concentrated, ruthlessly executed attacks. Dispersal reduces its striking power. Basic preparations for use at decisive points guarantee success.

Tiger battalions are independent units. They will be attached to other armoured units at the decisive point in the battle in order to force a result. They must not be used up too early by being employed for secondary tasks. They are especially suited to fighting heavy enemy tank forces and must seek this battle. The destruction of enemy tanks creates the conditions for our lighter tanks to carry out their allotted tasks successfully.

It is forbidden to assign missions to Tigers which can be carried out by lighter tanks or assault guns. Nor are they to be allocated reconnaissance or security missions. The Tiger battalion is organised as follows:

Battalion Headquarters (*Abteilungsstab*)
Headquarters Company (*Stabs-Kompanie*) with:
Signals Platoon (*Nachrichtens-Zug*)
Armoured Reconnaissance Platoon (*gepanzerte Aufklärungs-Zug*)
Scouting Platoon (*Erkundungs-Zug*)
Combat Engineering Platoon (*Pionier-Zug*)
Anti-aircraft Platoon (*Fleigerabwehr-Zug*)
Three [later, in some cases, four] Heavy Tank

Below: Tigers of the Waffen-SS's *Das Reich* Division rumble forward during the Battle of Kursk. Some units suffered heavy casualties: the 503rd Heavy Panzer Battalion lost nine of its 14 Tigers on the first day of the battle.

Above: At the sort of distances a Tiger could engage the enemy with its long-range cannon, even rudimentary camouflage, which broke up the tank's angular lines, was surprisingly effective, at least until the muzzle flash gave away its position.

Companies (*schwere Panzerkompanien*)
Tank Workshop Company (*Panzer-Werkstatt-Kompanie*)

B. Employment

In general, the same principles [which apply] for other panzer units are also applicable to the Tiger battalion. The following points are due to the special characteristics of the Tiger tank:

I. Marches

1. As the decisive-point weapon, the Tiger battalion is usually to be positioned towards the front of the order of march.

2. The march routes are to be especially carefully chosen.

3. The Battalion Commander is responsible for thorough scouting. Scouting and construction of bridges, fords and narrows on the line of march are especially important. Exact study of maps and careful interpretation of available aerial photographs, as well as timely deployment of the Scouting and Combat Engineering Platoons, are necessary.

4. During long marches, the Tiger units are not to be integrated into other armoured units, for technical reasons.

5. When crossing bridges the capacity of which is unknown or suspect, the lighter tanks and their combat supplies are to cross before the Tigers.

6. The average speed of the march during the day is 10–15kmph [6–9mph]; during the night, 7–10kmph [4.4–6mph].

7. Many maintenance halts are necessary during the march. Maintenance halts are to be ordered after the first 5km [three miles] and every 10–15km [6–9 miles] thereafter.

8. Roads with hard surfaces and high crowns [excessive camber] are to be avoided.

II. Preparing for action

1. To preserve the element of surprise, the assembly areas are to be [at some distance from] the enemy, because the howling of the Tigers' motors can be heard a long way. Pay attention to wind direction and strength.

2. After driving into the assembly area, the especially noticeable wide, deep tracks caused by the Tigers are to be eradicated to conceal the presence of heavy tanks from enemy aerial reconnaissance.

III. Combat

1. The Reconnaissance Platoon is to be sent in [ahead of the main force]. If required, light tanks can be assigned from the unit that is cooperating with the Tiger battalion.

2. In combat, the Tigers are to be sent into action at the decisive point. All other weapons support the battalion in the execution of its combat mission. Timely deployment of mine-clearing units and combat engineers, and close cooperation with them, is necessary to identify and clear mines and obstacles.

3. During fighting with enemy tanks, rapid handling and strict command are the prerequisites of success.

Commanders are to make repeated attempts to confuse and deceive the enemy by continually changing the method of attack. From experience, the following methods have proved successful:

a. Tie down the enemy tanks with frontal fire from the lighter tank units, then the Tiger battalion can skirt around and attack them from the sides and rear.

b. In a hasty frontal or flanking attack, the Tigers achieve superiority with supporting fire from lighter tank units.

4. In fighting in built-up areas, the Tiger is not to be employed in house-to-house combat because of the large 'dead' areas where the crew cannot see, and [due to the length of] the gun. The same applies to combat in forests.

5. The Tiger is especially suitable for pursuit. Preplanned scouting and early stockpiling of fuel and ammunition are the prerequisites for this. [This author confesses himself entirely baffled by the last paragraph.]

IV. Repair services

Every possible rest period is to be afforded the Tiger battalion for maintenance.

After a long period in action, sufficient time must be given for basic care and overhaul in order for it to recover its full combat strength.

The repair services are to be broadly supported by all offices and commands.

There were four formations authorised for the Tiger platoon. Line abreast (*Linie*), with the Platoon Leader on the extreme right and the Section Leader two vehicles away, was used for assembly. File (*Reihe*), with the Platoon Leader at the head and the Section Leader in the third vehicle, was used both for assembly and for marching, the former with 10m (33ft) between vehicles, the latter at 25m (84ft) intervals. Double file (*Doppelreihe*), which for a platoon was actually a box formation, was used both for approach marches, over open country, and in the attack, with the Platoon Leader at the head of the right-hand file and the Section Leader alongside him. In combat, the files were to be 150m (165yds) apart and the lines 100m (110yds). The wedge (*Keil*) was the most often used attack formation, with the Platoon Leader and the Section Leader level and separated by 100m (110yds), and the second tank in each section 100m (110yds) behind and the same distance to right and left, respectively. Since, when combat started, the Platoon Leader was to move to a position within the formation from where he could make the best use possible of both terrain and situation, the chances of either double file or wedge staying intact for very long seemed slight.

There were five authorised formations for the Tiger company. The column (*Kolonne*), used for assembly, was essentially three platoon files side by side, with the Company Commander and his alternate vehicle at the head of the centre file. For marches an extended file was adopted. The Company Commander took the lead, followed by the second *Kompanie-Truppe* vehicle, with the three platoons strung out behind. For approach marches a company double file was adopted, with the third platoon alongside the first. The company wedge was essentially a wedge of wedges, with the company headquarters vehicles in the centre of the formation, in echelon behind the rearmost tanks of the first platoon and ahead of the lead tanks of the second and third platoons; as an alternative, the second and third platoons could form file or double file behind the company headquarters vehicles. The broad wedge (*Breitkeil*) was the company wedge in reverse, with two platoons up and one back, and the company headquarters vehicles in the centre

Below: Elements of the 2nd SS-Panzer Division *Das Reich* assembled in Russia in October, 1943. Note the great difference in size between the Tiger on the left and the PzKpfw IV, with the long 7.5cm gun to the right.

Above: If nothing else, the Tiger's almost-horizontal upper glacis plate made a spectacular saluting dais ... on this occasion for *SS-Obergruppenführer* Walter Krüger, as he reviewed Knight's Cross recipients following the Battle of Kharkov.

of the formation, in echelon ahead of the two lead tanks of the third platoon. Where the company found itself on an open flank, the third platoon would deploy in echelon to the open side. In either company wedge or broad wedge formation, the company occupied an area some 700m (765yds) across and 400m (440yds) deep.

Where Tigers operated independently, with less capable medium tanks in support, the wedge formation was favoured, with a single heavy tank at its point and medium tanks (and later PzKpfw V Panthers) making up the tail. This was modified as early as July 1943, into a 'bell'. This was essentially a tight arc or rounded wedge of medium tanks with a Tiger in its centre, where a bell would have its clapper.

Not unnaturally, the tactical directives were modified in light of experience, and particularly when it became apparent that far from being 'especially suitable for pursuit', the Tiger was actually at its best in an ambush position, picking off incoming enemy tanks at long range with its superior gun.

DESTRUCTION OF LOST TIGERS

One thing became obvious very early on: despite their high level of protection, the attrition rate among the heavy tanks was severe, particularly in difficult terrain, thanks to its mechanical deficiencies. Effective means of recovering disabled vehicles from the combat zone were desperately needed, and it was vital to have adequate supplies of spare parts

on hand so that disabled vehicles could be returned to combat readiness quickly and smoothly. The strict instruction that no Tiger was to fall into enemy hands added to the problem, of course, for it meant that even write-offs had to be recovered, so that their destruction could be assured (and so that they could be cannibalised for useable spares).

In Tunisia, in January 1943, the 501st Heavy Panzer Battalion went to extraordinary lengths to achieve this. The unit lost its first Tiger to artillery fire, a round passing through the rearmost roadwheel and pushing in the side armour, failing to penetrate but rupturing the fuel tank inside. The crew managed to drive the tank out of the combat area, but soon the petrol fumes caught fire, and the tank burned out completely. During the following night, two 18-tonne (17.7-ton) three-quarter tracked recovery tractors towed the tank out of sight of the enemy, where such parts as were salvageable were removed (including the turret), and then the remains were cut up so that nothing identifiable remained. Another Tiger disabled the same day was later recovered. It had been hit 24 times, and five rounds had penetrated the hull and turret sides. Significantly, all of them had hit head-on, at 90 degrees to the vertical, but, apart from the

radio, no vital part was damaged. All the hits had been achieved with 57mm anti-tank guns firing from a range of around 500m (550yds). All this information was vital to successful operation; after-action reports were in great demand, and their contents soon went towards modifying tactical doctrine. In the light of the tanks' vulnerability to broadside fire from relatively light anti-tank guns, for example, the flank attack principle was modified to recommend a sustained three-quarters or full-frontal assault, and the instruction to attack on as wide a front as possible was reinforced, with a rider added suggesting the distance between individual tanks in formation be doubled.

Inevitably, as soon as Tiger unit commanders began acquiring combat experience, debate began over the relative merits of different tactical schemes as well as over the interpretation of tactical doctrine. Often, the proposals revealed an ignorance of the necessity to save the Tigers for when the going got really tough, and showed a willingness to commit them to battle at the first sign of resistance – hardly a surprising tendency on the part of junior commanders, but one that had to be restrained.

Frequently, suggestions for alternative ways to employ heavy tanks brought a sharp rebuke from Berlin. For instance, the after-action report from the *Grossdeutschland* Division concerning its activities in the Ukraine, west of Kharkov, during a two-week period in mid-March 1943 – before the 14-tank company structure had been inaugurated – suggested issuing an additional three or four Tigers to each panzer battalion. The justification for this was that the heavy tanks were so good at breaking up well-dug-in anti-tank gun positions and

forcing enemy armour firing at long range to take evasive action. The Inspector-General of Armoured Forces didn't mince words in his reply: 'The proposal to issue three or four Tigers to every panzer battalion is decisively rejected. The Tiger is a decisive-point weapon within the armoured unit. Dispersing them into the armoured battalions is an idiotic squandering of this valuable equipment.' Guderian was clearly being disingenuous – the suggestion, after all, had been to issue additional tanks, not disperse those already available. But at a time when less than 200 Tigers had been produced and issued (and 30 had already been lost in action), it is not entirely surprising that such a request got short shrift.

OPERATIONAL DOCTRINE

A subsidiary report from the same period by the commander of the *Grossdeutschland* Division's Tiger company started off on the wrong foot by stating that since the Tiger was so well-armed and well-protected, it was self-evident that the Tiger company should always be employed as the lead element in any attack. Guderian was to have his say on this matter, too, but the initial, somewhat hedged, reaction came from Army Headquarters: 'Employing Tigers as the lead unit is not self-evidently correct. Situations will occur where this is necessary or useful. The controlling factors are the tasks and the number of operational Tigers [available]. If there are only nine Tigers in the division [as was the case in

Grossdeutschland at this time], their assignment to the point means that the Tigers will not be available when they are needed to attack enemy tanks. Losses will frequently occur due to mines and bridge failure, plus getting hung up in untraversable terrain. In addition, immobilised Tigers will frequently block the way.'

Guderian was rather more direct in a letter dated 14 May 1943, just a week before the pamphlets quoted above were issued. 'The Tiger unit is the most vaulable and strongest weapon in a panzer unit', he said. 'If it is used as the point unit, it will quickly bring localised success because of its high combat power. However ... the Tigers will suffer heavy breakdowns due to mines, hits and terrain obstacles. Therefore they will enter the decisive phase of the battle already greatly depleted.' Thus already, the emphasis was on seeing the Tiger as a precious resource, to be hoarded and expended only very carefully, and to be protected from unnecessary exposure. The problem lay in defining 'unnecessary', for it often had one meaning to the headquarters echelon and quite another to the combat troops at the forefront of the fighting.

Guderian and the unnamed staff officer were perfectly right, of course. The Tiger had been conceived as a response to the superior firepower and performance of the Russian

medium and heavy tanks. If it was unable to meet and defeat them at the decisive point in the battle for whatever reason, then the huge effort which had gone into producing the superior vehicle was entirely wasted. It was bad enough when the reason in question was mechanical failure, as it so often was, but quite another thing when the cause of the heavy tanks' unavailability was because they had been squandered on targets that did not warrant their attention.

Just how much success Guderian had in ensuring that Tigers were not put at risk unnecessarily can be judged from the performance of one company from the 503rd Heavy Panzer Battalion as it advanced in the forefront of III Panzer Corps on the first day of Operation *Zitadelle* in the Kursk salient on 5 July 1943. This time it was undetected mines, many of them German, laid without a proper record of their whereabouts, which disabled nine of the company's strength of 14 Tigers (four more were disabled by other means). This cost the Germans any chance of success in that sector, for, with their decisive-point weapon disabled, they were in as hopeless a situation as if the Tiger had never appeared on the battlefield. In all, 34 of the 44 operational Tigers in the 503rd Heavy Panzer Battalion fell out during the period 5–8 July. At midday on 8 July, 12 tanks were still out of action, two of them total write-offs.

THE PRICE OF POOR HANDLING

Had the unit in question stuck to tactical doctrine and operated 'by the book', with its combat engineers, instead of its heavy tanks, pushed well forward on foot and clearing mines assiduously, the situation would have been much less critical. The corps commander, General Breith, repeated the standing instructions yet again in a written directive to III Panzer Corps, issued after the battle, stressing the necessity for proper reconnaissance and preparation and for all units to act in support of the heavy tanks. His instructions were to be reiterated continually until the very end of the war, almost two years later, but still – and despite the severest punishments – the instructions were frequently disobeyed, with a resulting effect on the performance of the heavy tank battalions.

From first to last, if the Tiger was properly handled, it was a potential battle winner. In the right hands, like those of Michael Wittmann, Otto Carius and the other acknowledged Tiger 'aces', it was a truly devastating weapon – though it has to be said that 'aces' do tend to be laws unto themselves, and that authority tends to turn a blind eye to their less-than-strict adherence to doctrine when the results are so spectacular. But it was not invincible, by any means, and if it was handled poorly, and particularly if too much was demanded of it, it was vulnerable. In fairness, as time went on the Allies developed weapons which could hurt the Tiger at longer and longer ranges – the Sherman Firefly, with its British 17-pounder gun, was perhaps the most important of them on the Western Front, and the Josef Stalin heavy tanks on the Eastern Front did much the same job – and at the same time, the German Army and the Waffen-SS were being pressed harder and harder by foes who had massive numerical superiority. In the end, the Tiger was beaten by sheer weight of numbers, like its feline namesake brought down by packs of dogs.

Above: Heinz Guderian, Inspector-General of Armoured Forces, who was adamant that Tigers should not be used as point weapons, though his orders were often ignored by commanders on the ground.

CHAPTER 4

The Tiger Tank in Action

The Tiger's operational debut in September 1942 was hardly impressive, but the Red Army soon learned that in the right circumstances there was very little it could do to combat the new weapon. Now it was a race to equip Wehrmacht and Waffen-SS units in meaningful numbers before the Allies developed a defence...

Elements of *1 Kompanie/schwere Panzer Abteilung 502*, with four newly issued Tiger tanks (chassis numbers 250002 to 250005) left its depot at Fallingbostel, between Hannover and Hamburg, in the last week of August 1942, to begin the long journey east and north to the Leningrad area. It was to join Army Group North, which, since the earliest days of Operation 'Barbarossa' almost 15 months before, had singularly failed to make any impression on the defensive ring surrounding the Soviet Union's second city.

The unit's deployment was to have an inauspicious start. Even before it was loaded on the train, one of the brand-new tanks' transmissions had failed; it was taken along anyway, and repaired in Russia. Two more were to go the same way almost as soon as they arrived, on 29 August. Thus, it was 16 September before the company – by now grown to two platoons with the addition of four PzKpfw III (75)s – first went into combat, against Soviet infantry and artillery in prepared defensive positions. The action was indecisive, and all four Tigers returned unscathed, their crews more confident than ever about the superior protection and firepower of their new vehicles. That confidence was soon to be shaken.

The second time the company went into action, on 21 September, the heavy tank crews immediately found themselves in difficulties due to the terrain – swampy ground, thickly covered with immature trees – which limited their mobility considerably. Three of the four tanks took hits from anti-tank guns on their own main armament, putting them out of the fight. One of them then burned out and, worse still, became immovably stuck in the bog. (It stayed there, defying all attempts to recover it, until 17 January 1943, when the Germans were forced to pull back from the area,

Left: The tide of war in the east, which turned at Stalingrad, began to ebb fast at Kursk. Most of these early Tigers of the Das Reich Division's schwere Kompanie managed to extricate themselves from the failed offensive. Note the Operation Zitadelle tactical symbol on the tank's front plate.

Above: The first Tiger to fall into British hands, Tunisia, January 1943. It took three hits from an anti-tank gun into the turret, all of which penetrated and caused the ammuntion to cook off. It was later the subject of ad hoc firing trials, which helped to determine Allied anti-tank strategy in the years to come.

Left: All the Tigers sent to Tunisia to fight the dual threat of the Allies advancing from both sides were lost, a number falling intact into British hands. While this tank shows no tactical number, it is conceivable that it is 131, which served with *1.Kp/s.Pz-Abt. 504* and is now to be found in the British Army's Tank Museum.

and blew it up to stop it falling into enemy hands.) The only bright spot in the operation was the complete failure of the Soviet anti-tank guns to penetrate the Tigers' armour.

The following week most of the rest of the company arrived, with three more Tigers, five more PzKpfw III (75)s and nine PzKpfw IIIs with the L/60 5cm gun. The remaining two Tigers, which had initially been issued to the battalion's 2 Company, and had later been transferred, did not arrive until mid-November.

It was January 1943 before they went into action again, and this time – operating against Soviet tank concentrations for the first time – they had mixed fortunes. In all, in the course of three separate operations between 12 January and 31 March, the company lost nine Tigers and 13 PzKpfw IIIs. (Six heavy and 12 medium tanks were lost in the first phase of the operation, which lasted three weeks; after that, no more than four heavy and three medium tanks were ever deployed at any one time.) In all, one-third of the medium tanks and one half of the Tigers were lost due to enemy action, the remainder succumbing to mechanical failure or becoming irretrievably bogged down. But on the other hand, 1 Company/502nd Heavy Panzer Battalion, destroyed some 160 Soviet tanks in that period – a very significant kill/loss ratio.

IN ENEMY HANDS

There was, however, the seed of a much more major setback hidden in those figures. One of the lost Tigers – and to make matters worse, it was the company commander's – was captured undamaged by Soviet troops on 16 January, after its driver ran into a bog. Russian engineers managed to recover it, and it was soon on its way east. By May, the Red Army knew everything there was to know about the Tiger's strengths and weaknesses.

Just as the Germans had realised, on examining a captured T-34 back in November 1941, that much of their inventory

Above: Tanks of *s.Pz-Abt. 503* first went into combat on 5 January 1943 near Rostov-on-Don, and spent the next year there before being decimated by the enemy during March and April 1944. Here, one of the battalion's companies breasts a steep hill on the approach march to yet another combat engagement.

of armoured vehicles was obsolete, so the Russians now came to the same conclusion. Their response was more appropriate – they fitted a much more powerful 85mm gun (as in the PaK/KwK 36, it was derived from an anti-aircraft gun) into the spacious turret of the existing KV-1 heavy tank and fitted that onto the hull of the T-34. The result was that the T-34/85 was probably the best all-round tank of its day. It was not always a match for the Tiger, but since its 9.36kg (20.5lb) APCBC rounds, fired at a muzzle velocity of 800m/sec (2625ft/sec), could pierce 100mm (4in) of armour at 1000m (1100yds), it certainly removed any presumption of superiority the German tankers may have felt.

Meanwhile, the 501st Heavy Panzer Battalion, which had been allocated Porsche Tigers, and had been promised to Erwin Rommel for the North African campaign, was in the midst of a hurried retraining programme to convert to the Henschel tank following the cancellation of the PzKpfw VI(P). The first two vehicles were received in September 1942. Eight more followed the next month, and on 2 November, because of British and Commonwealth successes at El Alamein, the battalion was ordered to North Africa, to join what was to become von Arnim's 5th Panzer Army as part of the 10th Panzer Division. In the period between the orders being cut and the despatch of the units, however, the situation changed dramatically as a result of Operation

'Torch', the Allied landings to the rear of the Germans, in Morocco and Algeria.

TIGERS TO TUNISIA

In response, and in order to reinforce Axis forces in North Africa, Hitler ordered the occupation of so-called Vichy France, which was unoccupied but under effective German control since June 1940. One of the panzer units ordered there was 2 Company/501st Heavy Panzer Battalion, which started its move to North Africa only at the end of the year. Thus, the entire battalion did not assemble until late January 1943, the 20 Tigers having arrived in Bizerta and Tunis piecemeal – between 23 November 1942 and 24 January 1943.

Intended originally to augment the troops trying to stem the British advance westwards through Libya, the tanks were actually just in time to confront the 85,000 Allied troops advancing from the west in the aftermath of the 'Torch' landings. Organised along with other units from medium panzer battalions as Battle Group (*Kampfgruppe*) Lüder, named after the 501st's commander, the battalion's first units, elements of battalion headquarters, headquarters company and 1 Company, became operational on 1 December. Between then and 13 May, when the remnants of the battalion surrendered, there were never more than 14 Tigers operational at any one time.

REINFORCING DEFEAT

Until the end of March these were the only Tigers operational in North Africa. During April, however, they were joined by battalion headquarters, headquarters company and 1 Company of the 504th Heavy Panzer Battalion, which had been formed in January, with a total of 11 more heavy tanks as well as its PzKpfw IIIs. (The 504th's 2 Company stayed behind in Sicily and was squandered there, as described later.) By that time the 501st had lost nine Tigers as total write-offs and had received no replacements, so the potential total strength of the two reduced battalions combined was only 22 heavy tanks, and actual availability only reached double figures once, in early April.

It is clear from the statistics that the Tigers played a significant – though by no means overwhelming – part in the Germans' attempts to hold on to their last foothold in Africa throughout late 1942 and early 1943. In order to make the most of the tanks, it was necessary to move them frequently around the combat area. But rough, mountainous terrain, a poor road system and wet winter weather, took a toll on the heavy tanks' running gear. That, rather than enemy action, accounted for the large number of vehicles rendered non-operational at any one time. However, newly arrived Tigers often needed at least a week, sometimes two, in the workshops to rectify mechanical faults, which only came to light after the tanks had been driven a few hundred kilometres. In fact, the first total loss of a Tiger did not occur until 25 January and a second total loss followed soon after.

The tank battles in Tunisia were the first encounter the Tiger had had with American and British tanks, though the German Army as a whole had had significant experience in Egypt and Libya. American light M2 Stuarts and medium M3 Grants and Lees had all long been available to the British, operating alongside Churchills, Crusaders and

Above: The distinctive radio antenna of this late-model Tiger reveals it to be a *Befehlswagen* command tank, equipped with extra communications sets to allow its occupants to talk to the higher echelon and to support arms. This would have made it the target of choice of every Allied gunner in the vicinity.

Valentines, and had not always proved a match for the PzKpfw IIIs and IVs. They were joined by the much better M4 Shermans in September 1942, just in time for the turning-point Battle of El Alamein.

The new American tank was first committed in the Western offensive in Tunisia in late November, with 2nd Battalion/13th US Armored Regiment. Reading American after-action reports against German records, the Sherman's first encounter with a Tiger seems to have taken place on 6 December, in the vicinity of El Bathan and Tebourba, when five Shermans were lost in as many minutes after encountering three Tigers and four PzKpfw IIIs of the 10th Panzer Division. Despite the superiority of the Tiger, however, there were scarcely enough of them available to make a difference, and the result was a gradual wearing-down of the German defences as the Allies' superior numbers began to tell.

Then, in February, the Allied attack seemed to lose steam, and the Germans mounted a series of counteroffensives. One of these, Operation *Frühlingserwachen*, began on St Valentine's Day, in the opening stages of what was to become known as the Battle of Kasserine Pass. The 10th Panzer Division attacked enemy concentrations around Sidi Bou Zid, in central Tunisia, from the north, while the 21st Panzer Division, part of Rommel's Africa Panzer Army, on the run before the advancing British, though in anything but disarray, attacked from the south. The 11 Tigers available that day came in from the east, along the road from Sfax, and now, for the first time in the theatre, they were able to manoeuvre more easily in relatively open terrain. On the first day of the operation, 3rd Battalion/1st US Armored Regiment lost 44 M4 Sherman tanks out of the 50 deployed – 15 of them to the 501st Heavy Panzer Battalion. On the next day, with the 501st's tanks held in reserve, the US regiment's 2nd Battalion lost 46 M4s, together with an M3 Lee. The American medium tanks, even with their improved M3 75mm guns, proved to be totally outclassed, not just by the 8.8cm KwK 36 but also by the 7.5cm KwK 40 L/43.

OPERATION *OCHSENKOPF*

The next major operation in which the 501st Heavy Panzer Battalion fought was Operation *Ochsenkopf* ('Oxhead'). The battalion was now temporarily renamed 7 and 8 Company/3rd Battalion/7th Panzer Regiment, and reinforced by the addition of 15 PzKpfw IV Ausf Gs, with 7.5cm KwK 40 L/43 guns, also known as PzKpfw IV Lg. Operation *Ochsenkopf* was an attempt to gain control of the mountain passes near Beja. This time, in more difficult terrain, the result was very different. At 0600 hours on 26 February,

Below: These two late-model Tigers, probably photographed in Russia in late 1944, show signs of suspension collapse, typical of damage inflicted by anti-tank mines. In too many engagements (particularly Operation *Zitadelle*), incomplete mine-clearing cost the Wehrmacht and Waffen-SS heavy tank units dearly.

Above: During the fighting in Russia in 1943, a new breed of tankers emerged, men who destroyed hundreds of enemy tanks. One such was Michael Wittmann (far left), next to Balthasar Woll, his gunner and – unusually for an enlisted man – a Knight's Cross holder. Note the victory rings on the gun tube of Wittman's Tiger.

when the operation began, Lüder reported 14 Tiger, 12 PzKpfw IV Lg and 15 PzKpfw III Kz tanks available. By the early evening of 1 March, all the Tigers, all but one of the PzKpfw IV Lgs and four PzKpfw III Kzs were unserviceable, many of them either total write-offs or lying in unrecoverable positions in the front line. Lüder's report that evening stated that none of the Tiger losses was attributable to mechanical or design deficiencies, but that weather and terrain (heavy rain on apparently bottomless ground) had forced his tanks to operate over a very narrow front, where they immediately ran into minefields. Effective artillery and anti-tank fire followed, while enemy infantry held off German ground forces. Significantly, no mention is made of effective action by Allied tanks. In the event, seven Tigers were lost – a very considerable blow.

AGAINST THE ODDS

The 501st Heavy Panzer Battalion – by now back with its own identity, but reduced to one company – and 504th were combined into a single command in mid-April, and were still managing to put up a good fight against mounting odds. They destroyed upwards of 75 Allied tanks between 20 and 24 April, for example. But by now it had become clear that no matter how powerful a fighting machine an individual Tiger was, it could not prevail against huge numerical superiority. By 4 May, when the last report of the operational strength of panzer units in North Africa was compiled, just one Tiger was serviceable.

One of the lost Tigers, which served in 2 Platoon/1 Company/504th Heavy Panzer Battalion, became more

famous by falling almost intact into British hands, than ever it did in service. Disabled by a round from a Churchill tank's six-pounder main gun, it was quickly abandoned. After a chequered career as show piece and test piece, it finished up in the British Army's Tank Museum at Bovington in Dorset, where it now rests.

EXTINCT IN AFRICA

The remnants of the 501st and 504th Heavy Panzer Battalions surrendered, along with the rest of the Axis troops left in Tunisia, on 13 May 1943, bringing the North African campaign. Thus, after a brief though often illustrious career, the Tiger became extinct in Africa.

Even as the first Tigers were going into combat in North Africa, the situation in and around the city of Stalingrad, was rapidly becoming untenable for Paulus's enveloped Sixth Army. To try to break the deadlock and contain the Soviet counteroffensive, heavy armoured units were rushed east. The 503rd Heavy Panzer Battalion with 2 Company/502nd Heavy Panzer Battalion attached – a force comprising 29 Tiger tanks and 35 PzKpfw III Kzs – was the first to be despatched. The first elements of the reinforced battalion arrived in Proletarskaya on New Year's day 1943, and by 6 January the move was complete, though the 503rd's 20

Tigers had actually gone into action the previous day. By the evening of 6 January, the score stood at 18 Soviet tanks destroyed (of which 14 were reckoned to have been T-34s) against one Tiger destroyed and 10 others rendered temporarily *hors de combat* through battle damage or mechanical breakdown. The relatively poor performance of the Tigers was put down to poor combat experience on the Eastern Front and unfamiliarity with the vehicles. Like the 501st Heavy Panzer Battalion, the 503rd had been trained on Porsche Tigers, and had only had a short time to get used to Henschel tanks.

Expensive as it was, in tactical terms the action was a success, for a strong Soviet armoured force was prevented from breaking through to the German railhead, where 2 Company/502nd Heavy Panzer Battalion was detraining after an eight-day journey from Fallingbostel. This unit went into action with the 17th Panzer Division on 8 January, after a 107km (67-mile) march. It joined up with the 503rd Battalion on 12 January, and was renamed as its 3 Company on 12 February.

In the meantime, the 503rd Heavy Panzer Battalion was so badly mauled – two Tigers destroyed, three more sent back to Germany too badly damaged to be repaired at the front, and only two in operation – that the whole battalion was pulled out on 22 January and sent to Rostov to rest. The respite was short, for by now the advancing Red Army had built up a considerable head of steam. On 2 February, orders to evacuate Rostov were given. Six Tigers (and 15 medium tanks) had been returned to serviceable condition by this time, but the remaining 10, along with three PzKpfw IIIs, had to be loaded aboard trains for transport further west. The operational Tigers of 1 Company were distributed between 2 Company and 2 Company/502nd Heavy Panzer

Battalion, which were now able to muster nine Tigers and eight PzKpfw IIIs, and eight Tigers and eight medium tanks, respectively.

By the morning of 8 February, the Red Army had entered Rostov and was fighting through the city, with the important railway junction of Zapadny one of its objectives. It was here the the German heavy tanks were concentrated, faced with some of the worst terrain imaginable for Tigers – narrow streets, littered with a maze of anti-tank ditches, most of them drifted over with snow and thus invisible, and everything covered with ice in the bitter mid-winter weather. To make matters worse for the Tigers' crews, the cabin heaters had to be removed, for they boosted the interior temperature to a point where the tanks' engines began to overheat. Conditions were tolerable when the engines were running, but wholly inadequate when they were not.

SUCCESS IN RUSSIA

In the event, the brunt of the fighting that day fell on the battalion's Light Company, while the Heavy Companies were reorganised to form an armoured spearhead for Battle Group *Sander*, tasked with fighting around the western edge of Rostov to link up with Battle Group *von Winnig* to the south, so that the two could turn east and re-establish the battle line. The main obstacle to this would be the huge River Don, and it soon became clear that the steep, ice-covered streets leading down to the river were impassable to the heavy tanks, while

Below: More often than not, tanks and infantry must work in close cooperation to guarantee each other's security. Here, panzergrenadiers discuss tactics with a tank commander before the start of Operation *Zitadelle* in the summer of 1943.

Above: Planning and discussion over, the panzergrenadiers move off towards the start line, while the Tiger stays in its hull-down position. The 'S' prefix to the tactical number and the (rather indistinct) twin crossed bars on the front plate of the tank reveal this to be a unit from the *Das Reich* Division.

the urban terrain made movement in tactical formation and adequate command and control next to impossible. To add to the difficulty, the supporting infantry – who were to have provided security in an environment where attack by enemy sappers carrying satchel charges was all too easy – were reluctant to leave the cover of the tanks, and were bunched thickly instead of spreading out to clear the houses. Inevitably, the attack ground to a halt over the next four days, though since the Soviet forces were subject to the same appalling conditions, no further ground was lost either.

This fairly bald account of a month's action on the Eastern Front in the depths of winter – the weather being the Soviet Union's most powerful ally – nonetheless gives a feel for the immense difficulties of fighting in such conditions. During all that time, the reinforced 503rd Heavy Panzer Battalion was the only unit in the sector operating heavy tanks. But during the latter part of February, the three Tiger-equipped Waffen-SS divisions (*Leibstandarte SS Adolf Hitler, Das Reich* and *Totenkopf*) together with the army's *Grossdeutschland* Panzer Division, each with one company of heavy tanks, were sent east too. All four were employed in the counteroffensive around Kharkov, which stopped the Russians in their tracks and stabilised the situation until mid-summer and beyond.

A DECISIVE VICTORY

German superiority at Kharkov can be gauged by a slice through the statistics. Between 7 and 20 March, the *Grossdeutschland* Panzer Division accounted for 250 T-34s,

16 T-60/T-70s and three KV-1s, at a total cost of one PzKpfw III, 12 PzKpfw IVs and one PzKpfw VI. The brunt of the fighting was borne by the PzKpfw IVs, as the losses for that tank indicate, but such a loss was understandable since in terms of numbers, those tanks made up some 70 per cent of the entire force. They accounted for 188 of all the Soviet tanks destroyed, while the Tigers got 30. In the lull which followed the fighting at Kharkov, another army Tiger unit – the battalion HQ, company HQ and 1 and 2 Companies/505th Heavy Panzer Battalion, which was created on 12 February, was also sent east, along with more than 1000 other tanks. It was not committed to action immediately, but instead continued with its training programme in the build-up towards the German summer offensive at Kursk – Operation *Zitadelle*.

During its strike west, the Red Army had created a semi-circular salient some 150km (93 miles) in diameter, centred roughly on the city of Kursk. In fact, in the sector which stretched from Kirov in the north to Belgorod in the south, the front described an inverted 'S', the Germans having hung on to the city of Orel, north of Kursk, and formed a salient centred on it. The German plan for *Zitadelle* was to pinch off the Kursk salient by striking south and north from its extremities, and to that end, over the course of the spring a force of some 37 divisions was established. Included in that figure were 17 armoured divisions. Between them they mustered 2475 tanks of all sorts, including obsolete PzKpfw IIs, command tanks of all sorts, flamethrower tanks and assault tanks but not including tank hunters.

THE BATTLE OF KURSK

It is reckoned that almost 1700 gun tanks were operational at the start of the operation at dawn on 5 July, 133 of which were PzKpfw VI Tigers. To these were added the 14 Tigers of 3 Company/505th Heavy Panzer Battalion, which arrived in the combat zone on the third day of the battle, as well as five tanks which arrived as replacements for those which *Leibstandarte SS Adolf Hitler* lost in action. A total of just 310 Tiger tanks had been issued by that time, so the number committed at Kursk represents a sizeable fraction. The only Tiger unit at full strength was the 503rd Battalion, now built up again after its losses before Stalingrad, and augmented to the standard of 45 tanks per battalion – as were the Waffen-SS Tiger companies and that of *Grossdeutschland* Panzer Regiment. But despite Heinz Guderian's advice that this unit, at least, should be deployed together, its three companies were divided between the 6th, 7th and 19th Panzer Divisions in III Panzer Corps. Thus, all the heavy tanks were allocated to Army Group South, whose attack was to be launched from the south, in the Belgorod sector, and were grouped in nothing more than company strength.

As it turned out, Operation *Zitadelle* was a disaster for the Germans. Throughout the spring, the Russians under Zhukov and Vasilevsky, two of the Red Army's most able commanders, had moved an estimated half million railway waggons of supplies into the salient, turning it into a massive

Above: A very rare picture of a Tiger a split-second after firing its main gun. The muzzle blast kicked up vast quantities of dust and debris in dry conditions, and this, as much as the flash itself, was likely to give away the tank's position to the enemy. The dust also prevented the gunner from getting off a quick second shot. The blast deflector at the muzzle went some way to alleviating the situation, but it couldn't prevent it completely.

Below: The destructive force of the Tiger's gun is vividly apparent here during an engagement on the Eastern Front. Smoke and flames shoot high into the air from the burning village, but the Tiger presses on, apparently unconcerned, intent on searching out its next victim.

strongpoint in the process. That they had the time to do this was thanks largely to Field Marshall Walther Model, 'the Führer's Fireman', who was given command of the German forces. He convinced Hitler not to launch *Zitadelle* in May, as originally intended, but to wait until July, in order to build up his forces. Unlike Bernard Montgomery, who was noted for a similar cautious streak, Model got it wrong. Soviet tank forces were greater in number than those of the German Army, and had the advantage of being located in established defensive positions, supported by anti-tank guns and mine-fields. (As we have seen in Chapter 3, those minefields were to take a heavy toll, particularly when German tactical doctrine broke down.)

LOSSES AT KURSK

The Tigers performed well in general, but once again were simply not present in large enough numbers to make a difference – and suffered through being too dispersed, when they might conceivably have secured an important breakthrough. In all, 13 Tigers were said to have been written off during the battle, though the total was probably somewhat higher than this. Thirteen is a relatively insignificant loss when placed against the total German tank losses of 563 for the entire month of July. The total German losses for the battle of Kursk are usually wildly inflated; *Brassey's Battles*, for example, puts them at 2900, which is plainly impossible, since the Germans didn't have that many tanks in the entire theatre.

Withdrawn to Germany in July 1943, and hastily issued with new tanks (the 17 Tigers which were all the battalion had left after a long spell in Russia were distributed between the *Das Reich* and *Totenkopf* Divisions), 1 and 2 Companies, Heavy Tank Battalion, 1st SS Panzer Division *Leibstandarte SS Adolf Hitler* arrived in Northern Italy in August 1943 to take over security duties in the vital industrial belt and to guard the mountain passes which communicate with Austria. Some, like the unit pictured above, were comfortable in the towns and villages of the region, while others, like those shown below, camped beneath the Brenner Pass, and lived in rather more spartan surroundings. Either way, the assignment, which lasted two months, must have seemed like a rest cure after the Eastern Front.

The decisive tank-versus-tank engagement of the battle came on its penultimate day, 12 July, when II SS Panzer Corps crossed the final Soviet defensive trench line at Prokhorovka and encountered the Fifth Guards Tank Army. As many as 1200 tanks, three-quarters of them Soviet, were soon engaged, making it the biggest armoured battle ever fought until the Gulf War of 1991 – though whether that actually constituted a battle is another matter. II SS Panzer Corps gave better than it got, at least in numerical terms, but heavily outnumbered as it was, that counted for very little.

Hitler called off the offensive the next day, by which time the forces of Army Group Centre had penetrated no more than about 15km (9.3 miles) over a front some 40km (25 miles) wide, and those of Army Group South to a maximum depth of perhaps 50km (31 miles) along a front of similar length. But it was not yet over. The Red Army soon counterattacked decisively, and recaptured all the ground it had temporarily lost and much more, including Belgorod and Orel, and later Kharkov. This spelt the end of Hitler's adventures in Russia, and from then on the German Army was pushed relentlessly back through its own borders and on to eventual annihilation.

OUT OF AFRICA

Even as the fighting in the Kursk salient was reaching a peak, the Allied armies which had finally thrown Axis troops out of North Africa were poised to jump across to Sicily and begin what was to be a very long and arduous campaign to conquer Italy. From as early as mid-April, when it became

Above: A Tiger of the 1st Company, *s.Pz-Abt 508* on its way towards the Allied beachhead at Anzio-Nettuno in very wet conditions. The Tigers were completely ineffective under these conditions and were soon pulled back northwards. However, in May, after the Allies had broken out and taken Monte Cassino, the battalion was sent back into action – and lost no less than 40 tanks in the space of six weeks.

Below: Probably the most bizarre picture of a Tiger tank in existence! This late-model Tiger was almost certainly pushed off the road by a bulldozer after being disabled by a landmine (the left hand track is missing). At least the rather disconsolate-looking soldier propping it up managed to stay dry!

Camouflage schemes

2/S.PZ-ABT 502, SUMMER 1943

The factory finish ochre has been oversprayed with large areas of brown on this Tiger serving in Russia. It has a full complement of S-mine discharger cups.

S.PZ-ABT 502, EARLY SPRING 1943

This early model Tiger deployed to the Eastern Front retains the Feifel air filter system. The overall colour is yellow, which has been overpainted with green markings.

1/S.PZ-ABT 504, SPRING 1943

This Tiger served in Tunisia, though its overall olive green finish indicates it arrived late in Africa. The tank is fitted with the Feifel air filter system.

8/S.PZKP, 2ND SS PANZER DIVISION *DAS REICH*, FEBRUARY 1943

This tank is painted all-white to blend in with the landscape of a Russian winter. The S-mine dischargers, shown on the turret, were never popular with crews.

Above: The *Das Reich* Division's Panzers had a long way to travel (from Toulouse and Montauban, close to the Spanish border) to join in the efforts to repulse the Allied landings in Normandy. This late-model Tiger is somewhere between Paris and the battle area, during the second week of July 1944.

clear that the foothold in Africa was growing precarious, Berlin had ordered that at all times at least six Tigers must be stationed in Sicily. As a stop-gap, 2 Company/504th Heavy Panzer Battalion, which was nominally on its way to join the rest of the battalion in Tunisia, was retained there. Altogether, 17 Tigers came to be stationed in Sicily – the nine from the 504th Battalion were never to complete their journey and were soon augmented by the six originally earmarked for the task, while two additional tanks, intended as replacements for the 501st Battalion, were also retained. The history of the detachment is a short and sorry one.

Originally known as the 215th Panzer Battalion, the combined unit was reorganised as a standard company under Organisation Table 1176e, with three tanks in reserve, on 9 July 1943, and was immediately incorporated as an organic part of the *Hermann Göring* Panzer Division. At dawn the next day, the Allied invasion of Sicily began.

DEVASTATED IN SICILY

The reinforced Tiger company was attached to the *Henrice* Panzergrenadier Regiment, whose regimental commander knew little or nothing about deploying heavy tanks. Worse still, he declined to listen to the company commander, and as a result the Tiger company suffered heavy – and perhaps quite unnecessary – losses. During the first three days of fighting, no less than 10 tanks were lost, either becoming bogged down in terrain which had not been sufficiently

scouted, being disabled by battle damage or through mechanical breakdown. Infantry cover was poor or nonexistent, and none of the tanks could be recovered; where possible, they were blown up to prevent them from falling intact into enemy hands. Three more went the same way over the next week, by which time many more Tiger crewmen were being used as infantry in defence of the airfield at Gerbini than were being employed in the role for which they had been trained (a ludicrous waste of resources). During the pell-mell retreat northwards, which followed Hitler's decision to withdraw from the island on 27 July, three of the remaining four tanks broke down, and they too were blown up to prevent capture. In the end, just one of the original 17 Tigers survived to be transported across the Straits of Messina to the mainland.

The German evacuation of Sicily, which began on the evening of 11 August, was complete by the morning of 17 August. Long before then, orders creating a semi-autonomous two-platoon unit to be known as *Tigergruppe Meyer* had been issued, and the eight tanks which it was to operate left the ordnance depot at Sennelager, near Paderborn, by train on 28 July. *Tigergruppe Meyer* operated with a tank-hunter battalion until it was absorbed into the 508th Heavy Panzer Battalion in March 1944.

TIGERGRUPPE MEYER

The small unit, which was involved initially in trying to contain the Allied advance from the invasion beaches of Salerno north towards Naples, and then in pinning it down along the Gustav Line and around the beachhead later established at Anzio, lost not a single tank during its existence, and for most of the time it was able to field at least five vehicles – the exception was during its last two weeks, when all its Tigers were temporarily out of service. This is in stark contrast to the operational record of the unit into which it was absorbed, which managed to lose no fewer than 76 tanks in Italy between February 1944 and February 1945, when it was finally pulled out of the country.

Another Tiger-equipped unit was also rushed to Italy when it became clear that Sicily would fall – this time direct from fighting on the Eastern Front. Two companies of Waffen-SS tanks from *Leibstandarte SS Adolf Hitler*, together with 58 medium tanks and 71 PzKpfw V Panthers, were detached

Above: A mid-production Tiger (binocular gunsight and dished, rubber-tyred roadwheels, but late model cupola) of s.SS-Pz.Abt. 101. It is seen here on its way to Normandy around 10 June 1944. Many of the battalion's tanks broke down during this road march, and arrived late in the battle.

from the forces left in the Kursk salient as soon as it became clear that the battle there was lost. They were deployed in the mountainous region in the north of the country, being mostly concerned with disarming the surrendered Italian Army and guarding the border with Austria, as well as Italy's industrial heartland. None of the 27 heavy tanks in question saw action during the period up until mid-October, when the *Leibstandarte SS Adolf Hitler* was withdrawn and sent east again.

HEAVY LOSSES AFTER CASSINO

The 508th Heavy Panzer Battalion was created on 25 September 1943 from remnants of the 8th Panzer Regiment, most of which had surrendered at the fall of Tunisia. The unit moved to Italy in February 1944, and slowly worked up to an acceptable level of operational availability, though two tanks, both from 3 Company, were lost early on: one was burned out after fuel leaking from a faulty union was ignited by a discarded cigarette, and the other 'brewed up' when hit by anti-tank rounds. After that, all went well enough for the 508th Battalion until late May, when its 54 tanks (the battalion had been reinforced by the absorption of what had been *Tigergruppe Meyer*) were thrown into the battle to contain the break-out from the Anzio beachhead. Again, 3 Company took the brunt of it, and within 48 hours the unit had lost 15 of its 16 Tigers.

DISASTROUS MECHANICAL FAILURES

The account of the loss of these tanks reads like a bizarre mathematical puzzle. The company formed up in hull-down positions behind a railway embankment close to the Mussolini Canal, and engaged the oncoming Allied infantry with high explosive. They achieved some success, and subsequently advanced over the embankment, leaving three of their number behind, one with transmission failure and the others disabled due to their tracks riding up over the drive sprockets. All the other 13 tanks managed to dig the muzzles of their overhanging guns into the ground during the descent, which does not say much for the crews' ability to learn from each other's mistakes. This necessitated a halt in open ground, presumably under fire, while their crews cleared the blockage.

By the morning of 24 May five were disabled, though one, damaged by anti-tank gunfire, managed to limp back to the assembly point at Cori under its own power. Five of the remaining 11 continued to hold the enemy offensive at bay, and, in fact, the attacking Allied troops were driven back some 3km (1.8 miles) in this sector, losing a substantial, though unrecorded, number of Sherman tanks in the process. The other six were detailed to recover three more of the casualties; four of them broke down, at which point the original three were ordered to be destroyed along with the one remaining tank already disabled and abandoned. Two of the five tanks in action were now withdrawn, and with the two still operational but uncommitted tanks, attempted to recover the four which had newly broken down. All eight made it back to Cori, but by that time only one of the four towing tanks remained operational, making just four in all. Three of them were subsequently put out of action – one was disabled by anti-tank fire, and the other two suffered transmission failure – and were, in

MICHAEL WITTMANN AT VILLERS-BOCAGE

Michael Wittmann was a professional soldier who joined the German Army as an infantryman in 1934, at the age of 20. In 1937 he enrolled in the premier division of the Waffen-SS, the *Leibstandarte SS Adolf Hitler*, and by the outbreak of war in 1939 he was an *SS-Unterscharführer*, in command of an armoured car. In 1941 transferred to an assault gun unit in the Balkans, crossing with it into southern Russia during Operation 'Barbarossa'. Here he began his career as a famous destroyer of enemy armoured vehicles which was to see his final score reach a total of 138 enemy tanks (and 132 artillery pieces). But it was not until 1943 that he really came into his own – by now a twice-wounded junior officer, with an Iron Cross in both First and Second Class, and newly in command of one of the Tigers in what was then still the 1st SS Panzer Regiment.

Wittmannn fought through the victory at Kharkov, the failure to penetrate the salient at Kursk and the winter campaign which followed, during which he destroyed 19 Russian tanks and three heavy assault guns in one day, on 13 January 1944. For this action he was awarded the Knight's Cross and promoted to *SS-Obersturmführer*. He then returned to join the 101st SS Heavy Panzer Battalion, as it had now become, based northwest of Paris, where he was appointed commander of 2 Company in April.

On D-Day, 6 June, the battalion was ordered to Normandy. But, caught in an air raid, it was 10 June before a now reduced force arrived on the fringe of the combat zone. One of the tanks was commanded by *SS-Oberscharführer* Balthasar Woll, Wittmann's gunner throughout the Russian campaign and now a tank commander. Woll, who was an ace in his own right and also a Knight's Cross holder, no mean feat for an NCO, had taken up the position in his leader's tank himself.

On 12 June, Wittmann was ordered to take over a position northeast of Villers-Bocage to defend against a suspected British armoured thrust to the north. Wittmann's force consisted of six PzKpfw VIs and at least one PzKpfw IV. On his right he had 1 Company, under the command of *SS-Hauptsturmführer* Möbius.

At 0800 hours on 13 June, enemy armoured vehicles – A Squadron/3rd County of London Yeomanry, with Cromwell tanks and at least one Sherman Firefly, began advancing up the road, halting when they encountered no opposition. It appears that Wittmann now decided on a reconnaisance and cut around behind the 3rd County of London Yeomanry to enter the village proper. Almost immediately he came upon three of the four tanks and promptly knocked them out with 8.8cm gunfire. (The fourth British tank had pulled off the road into a garden, and both the commander, Captain Pat Dyas, and his gunner had to watch helplessly as Wittmann's Tiger, vulnerable at this distance in its side armour, passed close by.)

Wittmann proceeded into the centre of the village and engaged the tanks of B Squadron there, taking at least one round from one of the Squadron's Sherman Firefly tanks. At this point he reversed his track, and ran head-on into Dyas's tank, taking two ineffective rounds from its 75mm gun before despatching it.

Wittmann turned off the road, and continued back up the hill. He first destroyed the half-track which was bringing up the rear of the column, and then turned his attention on the A Squadron Fireflies. Then it was the turn of the rest of the squadron's vehicles. Slowly, Wittmann made his way the length of the column, shooting up all 25 vehicles before turning back towards the village, this time in the company of two more Tigers and a PzKpfw IV. But Wittmann walked straight into a trap, taking a disabling round from an anti-tank gun on his left-hand track.

Wittmann and his crew abandoned their vehicle, and the *SS-Obersturmführer*, realising that there was a chance to bring the British advance in the sector to a halt, set off on foot towards the Headquarters of the Panzer-Lehr Division, some 6km (3.7 miles) north. He returned with a company of PzKpfw IVs, which were soon reinforced by Möbius' Tigers, and had little problem in recapturing the village. Two days later, Wittmann was promoted again and awarded Swords to complement his Knight's Cross.

On 8 August, Wittmann took Cintheaux, on the Caen–Falaise road. But during the evening, he fell victim to a group of eight Shermans. He destroyed two and immobilised a third when his tank came under fire from the other five. There were no survivors, and Wittmann was buried with his crew, in a communal grave, in the hamlet of Gaumesnil. A week later, the Falaise Gap was closed, and soon after, all the other Tigers in the theatre shared Wittmann's fate.

their turn, blown up. In the meantime, the last operational tank also broke down, though it was subsequently recovered by two captured Shermans, sent down from Rome, 50km (30 miles) away to the northwest, for the purpose. They towed it in tandem, along the railway track. The remaining men of 3 Company – a majority of the original complement, since it had only been a costly exercise in terms of vehicles – retired from the field, leaving all its other Tigers behind.

LIMITED MODIFICATIONS

Allied engineers examined the remains of no less than 12 tanks abandoned in and around Cori on 5 August, by which time the area was far behind the frontline. They concluded that the Tiger was: 'not yet sufficiently developed to be considered a reliable vehicle for long marches. When pushed, as in retreat, these troubles [with the tanks' running gear] are too frequent and serious for the German maintenance and recovery organisation to deal with.' It is a judgement that holds up very well today.

As we have noted, no attempt was made to improve the poor performance of the Tiger's transmission or running gear. Indeed, neither was an attempt made for its successor, the King Tiger. However, the few modifications to the original specification which were made took place at around this time, when the tank's original Ausf H designation was changed to Ausf E. These included improving the protection to the turret roof, the replacement of the binocular gunner's sight with a monocular version, the provision of a mounting for an anti-aircraft machine gun on the revised cupola and the substitution of steel-tyred for rubber-tyred wheels. Perhaps the biggest change in the tanks' appearance, which had come about during 1943 in Russia, was the coating of the armour with *Zimmerit* paste, a plasticised paint thickened with copious quantities of sawdust, applied in a coat well over 10mm (.39in) thick, the purpose of which was to prevent magnetic mines from sticking. *Zimmerit* was applied with combed spreaders, and tanks coated in it are easily recognisable by their corrugated appearance.

Altogether, the 508th Heavy Panzer Battalion lost 40 Tigers in May and June, and received a total of 33 replacement tanks during that time. In addition, the reconstituted 504th Battalion, which was under orders to go east to Russia, was redirected, thanks to the intervention of Heinz Guderian, and arrived in Italy in the first week of June, just after the fall of Rome. It fared little better, and lost almost half its tanks during the course of the month, but received 12 more as replacements during July. By February 1945, when the 508th Battalion was withdrawn to be re-equipped, leaving behind with its sister-unit the 15 operational tanks it could still muster, the 504th Battalion had lost a further 14 vehicles, and thus never recovered anything like its full establishment strength, though it remained in Italy until the war's end.

THE INVASION OF FRANCE

Almost as Rome was falling to Mark Clark's advancing Americans, the act that most Germans had been dreading occurred – the Allies landed in Normandy. The main reason that they were able to get ashore in strength was the success of a disinformation programme which reinforced Hitler's own belief that the invasion would actually come in the Pas de Calais. Thanks largely to overwhelming Allied air superiority, it was some time before any substantial defensive force equipped with Tigers could be delivered to the theatre.

At the time of the invasion, just three Tigers were stationed in Normandy. (There were also five King Tigers, the first to come off the production lines at Kassel, but they were so unreliable that they had to be sent back to Germany rather than risk falling into enemy hands after breaking down.) The Tigers were with the 130th Panzer-Lehr Regiment as part of its radio-control unit, attached to the Panzer-Lehr Division. On 10 June they were joined by the leading elements of the 101st SS Heavy Panzer Battalion, newly returned from the Eastern Front with its mother-division, *Leibstandarte SS Adolf Hitler*.

THE 101ST HEAVY PANZER BATTALION

A succession of long road marches took its toll on the battalion's 45 heavy tanks, though enough were operational to make a difference to the combat balance almost immediately. For just three days later, at around 0800 hours on 13 June, *SS-Obersturmführer* Michael Wittmann won the swords to go with his Knight's Cross by destroying virtually the whole of two battalions of the British 22nd Armoured Brigade, one armoured, the other armoured infantry, just outside the village of Villers-Bocage (see box opposite). Within a fortnight, however, the battalion, by now fully committed, had lost 15 tanks destroyed and all its remaining vehicles were out of service in need of repair. It was 8 July before it went into action again, with 21 of its remaining 30 tanks, and it lost two more that day. Between then and mid-August, by which time the Germans had been pushed back east well across the Seine and south to the Loire, the 101st SS Heavy Panzer Battalion never fielded even half its nominal strength.

The next heavy tank units to arrive, both of them nominally at least at full strength, were the 503rd Heavy Panzer Battalion, with 33 Tigers and 12 King Tigers, and the 102nd SS Heavy Panzer Battalion with 45 Tigers. The SS Tigers came by rail, but the rest of the *Das Reich* Division of which it formed a part made a long road march north from the Toulouse region, during which it was involved in the infamous massacre at the village of Oradour-sur-Glane. The 102nd's heavy tanks required 10 trains to transport them. Seven had unloaded their vehicles, west of Paris, by 27 June, but it was 2 July before the entire complement had arrived, and they still had a considerable distance to travel on their own tracks. It was 10 July before the first elements entered the battle, and 10 days later 10 of its Tigers had still not arrived at the front. By that time, six Tigers had been lost, though three of them were subsequently recovered, and found to be repairable.

The 503rd Heavy Panzer Battalion was directed to Dreux, west of Paris, the first trains arriving on 29 June, the last on 6 July. Attached to the 21st Panzer Division when it arrived at the front, the first elements of the 503rd Battalion went into action on 11 July.

In all, during the fighting to contain the Allied armies in Normandy, up to the last days of July, a total of 23 Tigers were written off, including eight which were captured. Bad as this was, much worse was to come when the Allies broke out and started pushing the Germans back. By 20 August, all the rest of the Tigers in the west had been completely wiped out, most of them in the Falaise Pocket, most of these falling victim to fighter-bomber aircraft. Only the two units which had been hit hardest early on, and had been pulled out of the fight and issued with King Tigers – 1 Company/503rd Heavy Panzer Battalion and 1 Company/101st SS Heavy Panzer Battalion, each with 14 tanks – managed to withdraw their vehicles back to the line of the Seine. An analysis by Allied engineers of the 28 Tigers captured during this three-week period showed that the overwhelming majority (20 out of the 28 captured) had been demolished by their crews following mechanical breakdown of one sort or another.

The next time the Western Allies encountered Tigers was during the attempt to sieze a Rhine crossing at Arnhem, when British and Polish airborne forces had the misfortune to run up against the 506th Heavy Panzer Battalion. Having been re-formed at Paderborn, the 506th was training in the area with newly issued King Tigers, together with the 14 Tigers of the hastily thrown-together *Panzerkompanie Hummel* (see Chapter 3). Here, with nothing more effective than PIAT spring-powered spigot mortars, the men of the Airborne Brigade stood no chance against the German heavy tanks and were unable to inflict any lasting damage on them.

By late September, what had become a trickle of new Tigers from the Kassel factory had almost dried up completely. Just 44 PzKpfw VI Ausf Es were issued after 1 October 1944, and most of them went to the 507th Heavy Panzer Battalion and to the panzer regiment of the *Grossdeutschland* Division. Most of Henschel's increasingly limited resources were now concentrated on producing King Tigers – 183 of the 485 produced were issued in the last four months of 1944 – and the heavier, better armed and better-armoured tank began to play an increasingly important role, though badly damaged but repairable Tigers were still going back to Kassel for rebuilding.

DRIVEN BACK ON TWO FRONTS

By the start of Operation *Wacht am Rhein* (the Ardennes Offensive, which the Allies came to know as the Battle of the Bulge) on 16 December, there were only 35 Tigers available to go into action on the Western Front: 27 with the 301st Panzer Battalion, the radio-control unit which had recently been brought back from Russia, and eight with the 506th Heavy Panzer Battalion. The other heavy unit in the theatre, the 501st SS Heavy Panzer Battalion, as it was now called,

Below: The fighting in the close countryside of Normandy was nothing like that in Africa, Russia or Italy. Adversaries could come upon each other literally around any corner, and the invading armies used massive force whenever they could apply it, as the devasted hulk of this late-model Tiger demonstrates.

was armed exclusively with King Tigers by that time; and the 503rd Heavy Panzer Battalion, which was also now armed with King Tigers, had been sent east to Hungary in October. In all, a total of 123 German heavy tanks of all types, including eight Tiger assault tanks (*Sturmtiger*) with 38cm mortars, were assembled, of which 79 were operational. By the end of the failed counterattack, those numbers had dropped to 116 and 58 respectively. The total was further depleted when the 501st SS Heavy Panzer Battalion was transferred to the Eastern Front in February 1945.

By 15 March, just 15 active tanks, two of them King Tigers, were left with the regular army units facing the massed Allied armies poised to cross the Rhine. In fact, on that day just four of them were operational. However, an additional 13 King Tigers were on their way from Sennelager to join the 506th Heavy Panzer Battalion. Further reinforcements were also about to be despatched: the 507th Heavy Panzer Battalion, with 21 King Tigers, and depleted single companies from the 510th and 511th Battalions bringing 25 more. Apart from small combat units hastily assembled from training depots, these were the last Tigers available to the troops in the west.

THE LAST TIGERS

There were less than two months to go now before the war came to an end, and Germany was threatened on all sides.

Above: An overwhelming superiority of numbers eventually allowed the Allies to break out of the Normandy beachhead and to begin the push out to the north and east. M4 Shermans, like the tanks passing this wrecked Tiger, outnumbered their adversaries in the theatre but had to cope with fanatical resistance.

Below: The remains of the lost Tigers of Wittmann's *2.Kp/s.SS-Pz.Abt. 101* in Villers-Bocage after 266 bomber aircraft of the the Royal Air Force had dropped 1100 tonnes (1082 tons) of high explosive on the village from low altitude.

Invasion across its western and southern borders was imminent, but more fearsome by far than the advancing American, British and Commonwealth armies were the approaching Russians, and it was in the east that all the available remaining heavy tanks were concentrated. Ever since the failure of Operation *Zitadelle*, the Germans in Russia had been on the defensive, fighting what was essentially a long, drawn-out rearguard action. This should perhaps have been to the Tigers' advantage, since they were not being pushed back rapidly, and, given time to set up, they were particularly effective in well-selected defensive posi-

tions. However, yet again the Tigers were simply too thin on the ground to make a decisive difference to the course of events.

During the latter part of 1943, after Operation *Zitadelle*, much of the German heavy tank strength was sent east – seven battalions or part battalions, with a total of 238 Tigers arriving by the end of the year. But these tanks were never concentrated in any one place, and instead were distributed thinly among the three army groups, the Russian offensive being likely to come at any one of a dozen or more points at any given moment. In all, nine battalions were employed on

the Eastern Front during 1944 and 1945, though not all were present at the same time. The last battalions to be issued with PzKpfw VI Ausf E Tigers and the last to be created, the 510th Heavy Panzer Battalion, was finally despatched in July 1944.

The first King Tigers appeared on the Eastern Front the following month, during which the original Tiger production line was shut down. After that very few new or rebuilt Tigers were sent there as replacements – less than 20 in all, together with the 11 older tanks from the 29th Panzer Regiment, which had been assembled from training detach-

ments and arrived to reinforce the hastily created *Müncheberg* Panzer Division in March 1945. By this time the Germans were about to be pushed out of Poland and back within their own borders, as the Red Army advanced relentlessly. Losses were such that production at Kassel could not hope to keep pace, and slowly but surely the heavy tank battalions were whittled away until by the last month of the war there were fewer than 50 heavy tanks of all types operational on the Eastern Front.

FINIS GERMANIAE

Throughout the entire period, the fighting was cruel, but some periods were worse than others. Some units – notably the 501st, 505th and 506th Heavy Panzer Battalions – were entirely wiped out during the Russian summer offensive of 1944, and were reconstituted in their entirety. The 506th Battalion, which lost 45 new King Tigers in just seven days of fighting, was not returned to the Eastern Front, but was retained in the west instead. But both the 501st and 505th Battalions did return there, the 501st to be wiped out again and the 505th to be reduced to less than a dozen vehicles out of 45 by the time it was driven back into Germany in the last month of the war.

By the first week of May, with resistance centred on Berlin, and supplies fast running out, the power of the Tiger had been entirely broken. Nonetheless, in barely more than two and a half years of fighting, and despite being available only in very small numbers, it had forged for itself a reputation second to none, and had become a symbol of German military might. In many ways, it was the prototype of the main battle tanks which came after it, having proved very effectively that only a vehicle with the heaviest armour and the most powerful gun could survive on the modern battlefield – but only if it met other important criteria, and was adequately supported.

SUMMING UP

However, the Tiger was certainly inadequate in certain subsidiary areas, and that, above all, led to its downfall. Too heavy for its engine and transmission, it was ponderous; it suffered far too frequently from stress-related breakdowns; and it had poor fuel economy and a very restricted range. Much of its running gear was overcomplicated, making proper maintenance next to impossible under combat conditions. Its turret traverse was too slow, even when the hydraulic system was in use, and painfully slow in manual mode, making it difficult to acquire moving targets. The lack of stabilisation of its main armament meant that it could not fire with any real accuracy except when stationary. But apart from these seemingly extensive faults, the Tiger's protection was in fact second to none, and its main armament was undoubtedly the best gun of its type in existence, two important factors which combined to make it the most powerful and fearsome battlefield weapon of its day.

Left: Tigers move through a damaged German town in early 1945. In 1944-45 a total of nine Tiger battalions were employed against the Russians, though by the last month of the war in Europe, there were fewer than 50 heavy tanks of all types operational on the Eastern Front.

CHAPTER 5

Tiger Variants

Such a small number of Tiger tanks were produced that variants were few and far between. Apart from the 90 Porsche-designed Tigers, converted into spectacularly unsuccessful tank hunters, just 18 chassis were completed as assault tanks.

Some tanks – the M4 Sherman and the Churchill in particular – were used as the basis for a wide variety of vehicles, but the PzKpfw VI Tiger, because of its nature and the limited numbers produced, was not one of them.

There were only three true variants of the Henschel Tiger produced, of which the most common was the SdKfz 267 and 268 Tiger command tank (*Panzerbefehlswagen*). This was the standard gun tank, stripped of its coaxially mounted MG34 machine gun and ammunition stowage, with some of its main gun ammunition storage space converted to carry extra radio equipment – longer-range Fu7 and Fu8 sets – to provide communication with command echelon and with the Luftwaffe units which provided close air support. Unlike some German command tanks, the Tiger command tank was not stripped of its main armament, and so continued to function as a gun tank. However, the main priority of the crewmen occupying the gunner's and the loader's positions was the operation of the auxiliary radio sets, though they could still work the gun if necessary. Other German command tanks used the empty gun space to house a command board, and merely had a dummy gun tube fitted. All command tanks, however, were distinguished by the extra radio antennae they carried, and were always a priority target.

RECOVERING DAMAGED TIGERS

Although fraught with difficulties, the approved method of recovering a Tiger was to employ an 18-tonne (17.7-ton) three-quarter tracked tractor (*Zugkraftwagen*), or even two or three of them, linking them in tandem where more than one was required, and using two steel towing cables, which were stowed on the side decking of each tank. Experienced crews went into action with the cables ready fastened to the towing eyes, and rigged diagonally, to minimise yawing. Rigid, A-frame towbars were more effective at maintaining control of a heavy tank under tow, and were used whenever possible.

The nominal establishment for a heavy tank battalion was 13 tractors, but a full complement was often unavailable.

Left: Just 18 *Sturmmörser* assault tanks – Tiger chassis with fixed, box-like barbette superstructures, mounting a 38cm breech-loading mortar – were produced. Eight of these, one of which is shown here, were present during the Ardennes Offensive in the winter of 1944.

Sturmtiger

FACTS AND FIGURES

Crew	seven
Weight	66 tonnes (65 tons)
Hull length	6.3m (20.6ft)
Width	3.72m (12.2ft)
Height	2.85m (9.35ft)
Engine	Maybach HL230P45
Gearbox	eight forward, four reverse
Speed	40kmph (25mph)
Range	120km (75 miles)
Radio	FuG5
Main armament	one 38cm Stu M RW61 mortar
Secondary armament	one 7.92mm MG34 machine gun
Armour	rolled homogenous nickel-steel plate
Hull front	100m (3.94in)
Hull side	60mm (2.36in)
Hull rear	80mm (3.15in)
Hull top	25mm (.98in)

Jägdtiger

FACTS AND FIGURES

Crew	six
Weight	71 tonnes (70 tons)
Hull length	10.65m (35ft)
Width	3.63m (11.9ft)
Height	2.95m (9.68ft)
Engine	Maybach HL230P30
Gearbox	eight forward, four reverse
Speed	38kmph (23.75mph)
Range	170km (106 miles)
Radio	–
Main armament	one 12.8cm PaK44 L/55
Secondary armament (later)	two 7.92mm MG34 machine gun
Armour	rolled homogenous nickel-steel plate
Hull front	150m (5.9in)
Hull side	80mm (3.15in)
Hull rear	80mm (3.15in)
Hull top	40mm (1.57in)

The only recourse then was to employ operational Tigers to tow disabled tanks. This was not always a last resort, since there was an understandable readiness to use tanks, rather than the unarmoured tractors, to recover vehicles disabled within the enemy's field of fire. This practice led to the subsequent loss of dozens – perhaps even hundreds – of Tigers.

Where possible, captured enemy tanks were used as recovery tanks. A very few Tigers were also thus modified as *Bergepanzer* Tiger PzKpfw VI (SdKfz185) recovery vehicles.

ASSAULT TIGERS

From late 1943, 18 Tiger chassis were converted to carriers for 38cm assault mortars, and designated *Panzersturmmörser* Tiger, though more usually known as *Sturmtiger* (assault tiger). These vehicles had their turrets removed and a built-up fixed superstructure substituted. Derived from the barbettes fitted to self-propelled anti-tank guns, the structure had front and side walls angled at 30 degrees to the vertical. Their main armament was adjustable in elevation through an 85 degrees range, from horizontal up to almost vertical, and through 20 degrees in traverse, both adjustments being made manually, via a worm-and-wheel/rack and pinion drive, and was a radically different design from that of any similar projector seen before. It used a cunningly conceived obturator to deflect the propellant gases through the space left between gun tube and liner, expelling them through a perforated ring at the muzzle and thus eliminating much of the recoil.

Above: A very few Tigers were converted to the recovery role, with their armament removed and a winch fitted to the turret rear. Usually, the Wehrmacht and Waffen-SS preferred to adapt captured tanks to this role, and reserve the Tigers for the job they did best – fighting.

The 38cm assault mortar fired 330kg (725lb) HE projectiles, fitted with stabilising splines, out to a range of 6000m (6562yds). The projectiles were too heavy for the crew to lift, and a small demountable crane was used instead. Fully loaded, the *Sturmtiger* carried 13 rounds, one in the gun tube and a dozen more in the side panniers. The mortar tube could be loaded only at zero elevation and zero azimuth, so the rate of fire was quite low. The tube was lowered to the loading position, and the loading tray, which incorporated rollers, put in place. A fresh round was removed from its stowage rack with the aid of a winch mounted on fore and aft rails in the superstructure roof, presented to the breach and rammed home, whereupon the tube could be elevated and aimed again. The whole operation required four men, including the gunner, while the entire crew consisted of seven. A single 7.92mm MG34 machine gun was fitted in a ball mount in the front plate. It is said that the only useful employment the *Sturmtiger* ever found was in the destruction of the Warsaw ghetto, though eight were present during Operation *Wacht am Rhein*.

Apart from the Tiger command tank, the most numerous so-called variant of the Tiger tank was actually a very different animal indeed, being a modified version of the vehicle Ferdinand Porsche originally designed as a competitor to the successful submission from Henschel. Though outwardly similar to the PzKpfw VI, the VK4501(P) was essentially very different. It had a very much more complicated transmission system – its air-cooled petrol engine driving a generator to drive the tracks by means of two independent electric motors – and longitudinal torsion bar suspension.

A USE FOR THE PORSCHE TIGERS

It is said that Ferdinand Porsche – a very talented motor vehicle designer – had personal access to Hitler and more than a little influence on him, and that it was this alone which secured the production of 90 PzKpfw VI Ausf P Tiger chassis in 1942. In fact, it is more probable that there was actually little to chose between the rival designs from Porsche and Henschel. As the latter had no experience as a tank manufacturer, and since the new heavy tank was so vital to the war effort, it was decided that a limited order for Porsche tanks should be placed too, just in case Henschel's production line ran into trouble. It did not, and after the first batch no more Porsche Tigers were ever produced.

Only five vehicles were ever completed in the original form. All the rest were sent to the Alkett factory in Berlin-Spandau, where they were converted to become heavy tank hunters. The first modification was to strip out the expensive

dom came round to their way of thinking soon enough. It passed its operational trials in March 1943, and all existing examples were allocated to Operation *Zitadelle* four months later. Thanks to a failure to provide the *Elefant* with any defensive armament, it proved sickeningly vulnerable to Soviet sappers with their satchel charges, while its 20kmph (12mph) top speed made it impossibly slow. Owing largely to its 65-tonne (64-ton) all-up weight, its range was only 90km (55 miles).

The heavy tank hunters were even more prone to breakdowns than the Tiger proper; very few got out of the Kursk salient under their own power. Later models were fitted with a hull-mounted machine gun, but all those committed to combat were captured or destroyed. One encyclopedia of military technology describes the *Elefant* as 'an impractical combat weapon which well illustrates the dangers of designing armoured vehicles solely with an eye to theoretical advantages and without considering basic tactical demands'.

Despite its similar name, and the fact that it shared an engine and transmission system and was armed with an 8.8cm gun, the PzKpfw Tiger II Ausf B King Tiger was not a variant of the Tiger tank. Indeed, many would regard it as a heavyweight development of the PzKpfw V Panther instead.

The German heavy tank was quite different enough from the original PzKpfw VI Tiger to merit a comprehensive study

air-cooled engines, problems with which had threatened the Porsche project from the beginning, and replace them with Maybach HL230 powerplants, though retaining the electric drive. Then a new body, with a fixed superstructure in place of a turret, straight-set frontal armour 200mm (0.8in) thick and sloping 80mm (3.2in) armour in the sides and rear, was constructed. This was fitted with the L/71 PaK 43/2 gun (as later fitted to the King Tiger, in a slightly modified form) with only very limited traverse and elevation.

The new *Panzerjäger* Tiger (P) (SdKfz 184) was officially nicknamed *Ferdinand*, but the troops who were unfortunate enough to have to operate it called it the *Elefant*, and official-

Above: The Tiger was superseded by the heavier King Tiger. This early version with the turret designed by Porsche (note the under-cut lower face) has the more powerful L/71 KwK43 8.8cm gun and more resistant armour. But it had the same powerplant, and so was ponderous and only effective in a static defensive role.

of its own, though we may look at its main points here, if only to show in which direction trends in German heavy tank design were to go.

Most obviously, the designers acknowledged the fact that sloping armour provided enhanced protection. They angled the upper and lower front glacis plates of the new tank at 40 degrees, and the hull side plating at 60 degrees, carrying that

angle through into the sides of the completely redesigned turret, which incorporated a pronounced bustle at the rear to provide better ready storage for main gun ammunition, as well as what later came to be known as a ballistic form. They also upped the thickness of the armour plate itself, to a minimum of 40mm (1.5in) on the turret roof and the upper surface of the hull, and a maximum of 150mm (6in) in the upper front glacis and a massive 180mm (7.2in) on the turret face.

All this and the choice of a better 8.8cm gun, with a longer 71-calibre barrel pushed the all-up weight of the new tank, variously called the *Königstiger* and the Tiger II, and by the American and British soldiers who came up against it the Royal Tiger or King Tiger, to 70 tonnes (68.9 tons). Since

Below: The Panzerjäger Tiger *(P) (SdKfz 184)* Elefant, *which lacked any kind of secondary armament. As a result, in battle it proved to be vulnerable to troops armed with satchel charges, and suffered losses accordingly.*

Above: All the tanks Porsche persuaded the Wehrmacht to order were converted to become Jägdtiger *tank hunters. Extremely slow, and with an abysmal record of mechanical failure, they were doomed by a lack of defensive armament.*

the same HL 230 powerplant developed for the Tiger was chosen for the new heavy tank, its performance was less than sparkling – it was said to be able to attain 38kmph (24mph) on the road, but more realistically, could manage not much more than half of that across country – while its thirst for petrol was prodigious; even on the road its 865-litre (190-UK gal) tanks could only sustain it for 110km (70 miles).

Only 492 King Tigers were produced between January 1944, when the first five were despatched to the Panzer-Lehr Division in France, and March 1945, by which time Germany's industrial base was effectively destroyed. Production reached its peak in August 1944, when 94 tanks were rolled out of the Henschel factory. The operational inventory never exceeded 226, reached in February 1945.

PanzerKampfwagen VI Tiger Ausf H/E Specifications

Crew	Five
Hull length	6.3 m (20.66ft)
Length, gun forward	8.45m (27.7ft)
Width, combat tracks fitted	3.72m (12.2ft)
Width, transport tracks fitted	3.14m (10.3ft)
Height (to commander's hatch top)	3.0m (9.8ft)
Transportation weight	50.5 tonnes (49.7 tons)
Combat weight	57 tonnes (56 tons)
Ground pressure, combat tracks	1.04kg sq cm (14.8 psi)
Ground pressure, transport tracks	1.43kg sq cm (20.4 psi)
Ground clearance	0.47m (1.5ft)
Fording depth, without preparation	1.6m (5.24ft)
Fording depth, prepared	4m (13.1ft)
Maximum gradient	70 per cent
Maximum trench crossing	2.5m (8.2ft)
Maximum step climbing	0.8m (2.6ft)

Suspension type	Transverse torsion bars
Number of roadwheel sets	Eight per side
Roadwheel sets per torsion bar	One
Roadwheels per set	Three (outers removable; later two)
Return rollers	None
Wheel size	800 x 75mm (31.5 x 2.95in)
Tyres	Rubber (later composite rubber/steel)

Powerplant type	Maybach HL230 P45 petrol
Configuration	4-strokeV-12 @ 60 degrees; SOHC per bank
Valves	Two per cylinder; sodium cooled in exhaust
Material	Cast-aluminium crankcase and block; cast-iron heads
Nominal output	700hp @ 3000rpm
Nominal efficiency	30.4hp/litre
Power/weight ratio (combat)	12.3hp/tonne
Capacity	23095cc (1410 cu in)
Bore	130mm (5.118in)
Stroke	145mm (5.709in)
Compression ratio	6.8:1
Aspiration	Four twin-choke Solex type 52JFF
Crankshaft bearings	Seven, roller type
Lubrication system	Dry sump; two scavenger pumps, one pressure pump
Oil capacity	28 litres (6.16 UK gallons/7.4 US gallons)
Coolant type	Liquid, fan-assisted
Coolant capacity	75 litres (16.5 UK gallons/19.8 US gallons)
Fuel capacity	540 litres (118.8 UK gallons/142 US gallons)
Nominal range, road	195km (120 miles)
Nominal range, cross-country	110km (68 miles)
Nominal maximum speed	45.4kmph (28mph) (reduced to 38kmph (23mph) by limiting engine to 2500rpm

Average sustained road speed	40kmph (25mph)
Average cross-country speed	20kmph (12.5mph)
Transmission type	OLVAR hydraulically actuated pre-selector gearbox, 8 forward, 4 reverse speeds, hydraulically actuated clutch
Final drive	Epicyclic
Driven sprocket	Front

Maximum speed in gears

1st	2.8kmph (1.8mph)
2nd	4.3kmph (2.7mph)
3rd	6.2kmph (3.8mph)
4th	9.2kmph (5.7mph)
5th	14.1kmph (8.7mph)
6th	20.9kmph (13mph)
7th	30.5kmph (18.9mph)
8th	45.4kmphh (28mph)
1st reverse	2.8kmph (1.8mph)
2nd reverse	4.3kmph (2.7mph)
3rd reverse	6.2kmph (3.8mph)
4th reverse	9.2kmph (5.7mph)

Steering type	Wheel-controlled hydraulically operated regenerative; emergency steering by differential braking
Minimum turning radius	3.44m (11.28ft)
Maximum turning radius	165m (525ft)
Main armament	8.8cm L/56 KwK36 rifled cannon
Secondary armament	Two 7.92mm MG34 machine guns; one co-axially mounted, one hull mounted
Ancilliary armament	One 7.92mm MG34 AA machine gun (later optional) Six smoke dischargers (later removed) Three 92mm bomb/grenade launchers (later removed) One 9mm MP38 or MP40 machine pistol 9mm P38 pistols
Main armament ammunition	92 rounds (field-modified to 106/120 rounds in some cases)
Secondary armament ammunition	5100 rounds (34 belts of 150 rounds each)

Armour	Rolled homogenous nickel-steel plate; electro-welded interlocking-plate construction (dimensions are nominal)
Hull front	100mm (3.94in)
Hull side (upper)	80mm (3.15in)
Hull side (lower)	60mm (2.36in)
Hull rear	80mm (3.15in)
Hull top	25mm (0.98in)
Hull bottom	25mm (0.98in)
Turret front	100mm (3.94in)
Mantlet	120mm (4.72in)
Turret sides	80mm (3.15in)
Turret rear	80mm (3.15in)
Turret top	25mm (40-45mm) 0.98in (1.57-1.77in)

Turret traverse method	Hydraulic/manual
Traverse rate (maximum)	Six degrees/second
Elevation method	Manual
Elevation range	Plus 17 to minus 6.5 degrees
Stabilisation	None

The Tiger's Main Rivals

VEHICLE	SHERMAN M4	T34 - 76A	CROMWELL MK V
Crew	Five	Four	Five
Hull length	5.85m (19.2ft)	6.1m (20ft)	6.24m (20.47ft)
Length, gun forward	5.85m (19.2ft)	6.1m (20ft)	6.4m (21ft)
Width	2.62m (8.6ft)	3.0m (9.84ft)	3.05m (10ft)
Height (to hatch)	2.74m (8.98ft)	2.45m (8ft)	2.46m (8ft)
Weight	30.25 tonnes (29.77 tons)	26.5 tonnes (26 tons)	27.9 tonnes (27.45 tons)
Ground pressure (kg sq cm)	1.1	0.64	0.95
Fording capacity	1.0m (3.28ft)	1.1m (3.6ft)	0.9/1.22m (2.95/4ft)
Gradient	60 per cent	70 per cent	47 per cent
Trench	2.3m (7.54ft)	3.0m (9.84ft)	2.3m (7.54ft)
Step	0.6m (1.96ft)	0.9m (2.95ft)	0.9m (2.95ft)
Suspension type	Vehicle volute springs	Christie/coil springs	Christie/coil springs
Powerplant	R-975-C1 radial petrol	V-2-34 V-12 diesel	R-R Meteor V-12 petrol
Output	400hp	500hp	600hp
Power/weight ratio	13.22hp/tonne	19hp/tonne	21.5hp/tonne
Capacity	15900cc	38900cc	26900cc
Fuel capacity	660litres (174 gallons US)	420 litres (111 gallons US)	525 litres (138 gallons US)
Range, road	160km (100 miles)	450km (281 miles)	280km (175 miles)
Range, cross-country		260km (162.5 miles)	
Nominal maximun speed	35kmph (21.9mph)	47kmph (29.37mph)	62kmph (38.75mph)
Steering type	Cletrac	Clutches	Regenerative
Turning radius	9.5m (31.16ft)	3.8m (12.46ft)	In place
Main armament	75mm L/40 M3	76.2mm L/30.5 M1938	75mm L36.5 Mk V
Secondary armament	Two 0.3in M1919 MG	Two 7.62mm DT MG	Two 7.92mm Besa MG
Main armament ammunition	97 rounds	80 rounds	64 rounds (composite)
Secondary ammunition	4750 rounds	2400 rounds	4952 rounds
Armour	Cast/rolled, welded	Rolled, welded	Rolled, welded/riveted
Hull front	50.8mm (2in)	45mm (1.77in)	63mm (2.48in)
Hull sides	50.8mm (2in)	45mm (1.77in)	32mm (1.26in)
Hull rear	50.8mm (2in)	40mm (1.57in)	32mm (1.26in)
Hull top	19mm (.75in)	20mm (.78in)	20mm (.78in)
Hull bottom	19mm (.75in)	15mm (.59in)	14mm (.55in)
Turret front	76.2mm (3in)	45mm (1.77in)	76mm (2.3in)
Mantlet	90mm (3.54in)		
Turret sides	76.2mm (3in)	45mm (1.77in)	63mm (2.48in)
Turret rear	76.2mm (3in)	40mm (1.57in)	57mm (2.24in)
Turret top	25.4mm (1in)	15mm (.59in)	20mm (.78in)
Turret traverse	Hydraulic/manual	Electric/manual	Hydraulic/manual
Elevation range (degrees)	+25 to -10 degrees	+30 to -3 degrees	+20 to -12.5 degrees
Stabilisation	Elevation	None	None

PzKpfw VI Tiger Inventory

January 1943–February 1945

Total number available (whether actually operational or not)

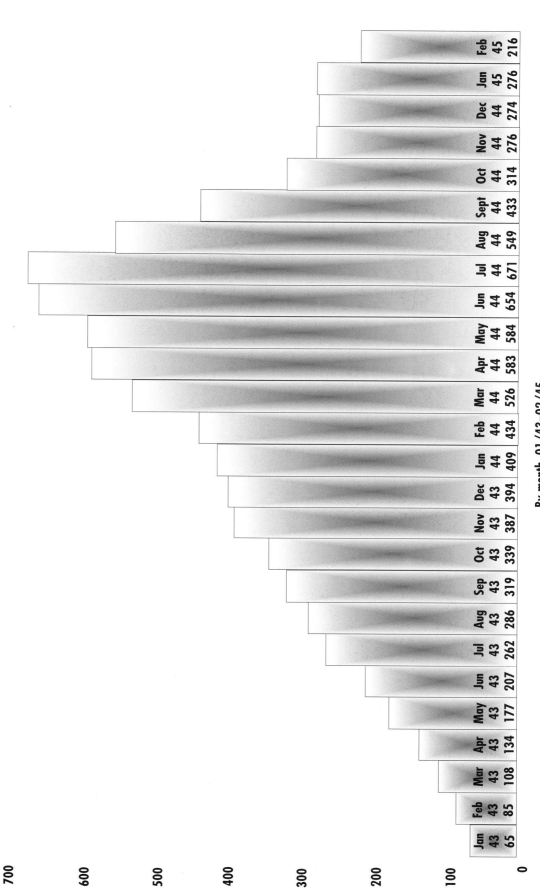

Number of vehicles available

	Jan 43	Feb 43	Mar 43	Apr 43	May 43	Jun 43	Jul 43	Aug 43	Sep 43	Oct 43	Nov 43	Dec 43	Jan 44	Feb 44	Mar 44	Apr 44	May 44	Jun 44	Jul 44	Aug 44	Sept 44	Oct 44	Nov 44	Dec 44	Jan 45	Feb 45
	65	85	108	134	177	207	262	286	319	339	387	394	409	434	526	583	584	654	671	549	433	314	276	274	276	216

By month, 01/43–02/45

INDEX